The Force of Tenderness

The Union of Spirit & Soul

DOROTHY J. AVERY

The Force
of Tenderness

The Union of Spirit & Soul

SOPHIA PERENNIS

Series Editor: James R. Wetmore

For information, address:
Sophia Perennis
34A Main St., Peterborough,
Peterborough, NH 03458
angelicopress.com

ISBN 978-1-59731-170-0 (pbk)

Cover Design: Michael Schrauzer
Cover Image: William Blake (1757–1827),
Pity (c. 1795) Yale Center for British Art

CONTENTS

Introduction 1

PART ONE
William Blake

1 *William Blake and Pity* 9
2 *Blake and the Feminine* 24

PART TWO
Woman as Goddess in Pre-History

3 *The Goddess, Woman, and Birth* 45
4 *The Goddess, Woman, and Death* 62

PART THREE
Woman and Goddess in Archaic Greece

5 *The Goddess, Woman, and Marriage in the* Iliad 77
6 *The Goddess, Woman, and Marriage in the* Odyssey . . 113

PART FOUR
Women's Diverging Roles

7 *The Iliadic and Odyssean Divergence* 145

Conclusion 173

ACKNOWLEDGMENTS

Gordon (1933–2001)
Roger Sworder, friend and mentor
Temenos Academy Review, for the reprinting
of 'William Blake on Pity'

Introduction

WITHIN THIS WORLD there is the most curious of opposites, woman–man. In Western culture, traditionally the woman is associated with the soul and the man with the spirit. William Blake's paradigmatic perception of marriage between woman and man—which he sees as uniting the soul with the spirit and as leading to union with the divine—is a traditional thought. Marriage is a transcendent and spiritual union. This union is not simply a psychological state, however profound, but a superhuman reality.

The absolute which Blake recognized is that soul and spirit, woman and man, are united through the emotion of pity—soul and spirit with the divine, and woman and man in *hieros gamos,* sacred marriage. The roles of male and female in our time are often fraught with difficulty and misunderstanding. There have been many attempts to rediscover an ideal past where the feminine role is more clearly defined and appreciated, but attempts of this kind have often manipulated such facts as we seem to have. I have chosen to use the work of Blake as a means to reinterpret the past, as he has a far surer understanding of the spiritual standings of both sexes than can be found in today's theorists. Obviously he did not drink of the waters of Lethe. There is no distinction between life and a life hereafter for Blake. I am aware that some critics will call this "pedestalian" thought, but the difference between this use of "pedestalian" thinking and most,[1] is that both sexes are to climb the pedestal. Blake's conception that man and woman are "undivided Essence" is the basis for this thesis. For the Oglala Lakota,

---

[1] Lillian E. Doherty, *Gender and the Interpretation of Classical Myth,* 2001, London, Gerald Duckworth, 115.

behind the woman's power of life is hidden the power of man . . . the woman is the life of the flowering tree, but the man must feed and care for it.[2]

Kabir expresses this same idea:

As the seed is with the banyan tree, and within the seed are the flowers, the fruits and the shade,
So the germ is within the body and within that germ is the body again. (XLVI)[3]

Neither the Oglala Lakota, Kabir, nor Blake are speaking of "getting in touch with your feminine or masculine side," as if this were merely a matter of power-dressing with shoulder pads or burping the baby. They are speaking of a deep spiritual recognition that this masculine/feminine division represents the spirit and the soul, and that they are present within both female and male. The manifest world, the garden, the flowering tree must naturally be the work of the feminine, as she is the part of the human equation able to make manifest. The realm of the spirit therefore must logically belong to those who do not possess the obvious qualities of making manifest—that is, the male. But both require the other and are, indeed, the "other" within themselves. To the female is attributed not only the power of increase but the potency that death and decay represent, which is union with the immutable. Again, this is a logical equation, because she—the female—is the material part of the partnership. Just as she is connected with creation, so must she be connected with its opposite—destruction, decrease, or death. To deny this attribute to that portion of the human equation is to deny the mutability within all humanity. It is the mutable quality of the soul and its relationship to the feminine that is problematic now.

The modern Western world seeks to make some kind of sense concerning the role of women, while yet undervaluing the ability to create life and denying the existence of death. Death, after all, cannot be seen as "progressive" by modern rational societies, for it is a physical finality. Our type of society is geared towards a

[2] John G. Neihardt, *Black Elk Speaks*, 1959, New York, Pocket Books, 178.
[3] Kabir, *Kabir's Poems*, trans. Tagore, 1915, London, MacMillan, 52.

progression that physically betters what we presently have in this world. Death cannot be seen as a progression in a society that emphasizes the values of getting and keeping material and physical health. Because we cannot easily reflect on death as the necessary corollary to life as our forefathers did, we are unable to see that this world—with its emphasis upon material achievements, youth, and fame—is ephemeral when compared to the wisdom of the poet's song.

To trace the perceptions of the feminine from pre-history, through Classical Greece, Blake has been the guide. Blake's very keen distress at the spiritual condition of his beloved Albion allows a pre-Enlightenment concept of the world to emerge. That he writes in response to the physical conditions occurring in his world is undeniable. But what is also undeniable is that he sees these physical losses as indicative of far greater losses. Kathleen Raine's *Blake and Tradition* traces the links from Blake's work back to traditional thought. S. Foster Damon's *A Blake Dictionary* is a sympathetic attempt to locate his prompts not only in the physical world but in the traditional world. Ellis and Yeats, who brought Blake back into the literature of England, are empathetic editors. More contemporary studies of Blake's work, however, tend to focus only on material prompts, to analyze the physical world that he inhabited, forgetting what Blake himself has said, "every thing that lives is holy!"[4] With this phrase in mind, the role of female and male in the physical world becomes transcendent. It is unlikely that Blake was familiar with Taoist philosophy, yet his understanding of female and male relations was as theirs.

> Here, dark (yin, feminine) and light (yang, masculine) are equally contained within a circle, divided by an S curve, each "half" containing a spot of the other's colour and nature. What is immediately apparent is that the black and the white are not divided down the middle with a straight line, so creating opposites that are clearly delineated and

[4] *Blake: Complete Writings*, ed. Keynes, 1989, Oxford, Oxford University Press, *VDA.* 8:10. Further quotations from Blake will use "K" followed by the page number, title, book or page number, and line number as shown on the abbreviations page.

absolute, but instead the distinction is provisional, alternating, continually in play. Each contains the other in embryo, and the force of the curve is to send the mind around the circle, and not to allow it to become fixed in one part or another, nor to begin at any particular place.[5]

Not "to begin at any particular place," but to accept that each is the other, both equal, both different, is the premise on which this thesis is established.

Consider the child, William Blake, a child who, according to his first biographer, Alexander Gilchrist, had already experienced visions, and his exposure to the glories of antiquity. His training, in the past and in learning his craft, included work on Bryant's *New System of Mythology.* Kathleen Raine says that the

> *Mythology* was a gold-mine, upon which Blake drew in the composition of his own pantheon of mythological lore; a universal language (as Bryant himself had understood) of the human imagination, with dialectical variations according to time, place, and local tradition.[6]

As a sixteen-year-old he became steeped in traditional thought when engaged in a "solitary study of authentic English history in stone."[7] Gilchrist tells us that he was often locked in, when the church was not in use, and "the spirit of the past became his familiar companion."[8] Throughout Blake's work, this "familiar companion" becomes a lens onto mythical and non-mythical places and peoples for us as well. Blake's position in history, standing as he does on the cusp of the Industrial Revolution, and the enormous breadth of traditional knowledge he possesses, show us what the loss of this time-honoured wisdom has brought. With Blake as guide, realization that "We are led to Believe a Lie When we see not Thro' the Eye,"[9] will help us mea-

---

[5] Anne Baring and Jules Cashford, *The Myth of the Goddess,* 1991, London, Penguin Books, 674.

[6] Kathleen Raine, *William Blake,* 1988, London, Thames & Hudson, p.15

[7] Alexander Gilchrist, *Life of William Blake,* 1942, London, J.M. Dent & Sons, 14.

[8] Gilchrist, ibid., 15.

[9] K.433, Aug:125.

sure the losses we have incurred. His singular position as modern mythographer, historian, and prophet will enable us to see how much our contemporary world has lost in our replacement of vision by sight.

The method chosen in this work is that of a close reading of the texts, in particular, those of Blake and Homer. Roger Sworder states that:

> Even in the later twentieth century there has been one great university exponent of the ancient philosophy, Kathleen Raine. Like Taylor, she has maintained the tradition almost alone in a hostile world. Yeats and Blake seem to have led her to Taylor, and Taylor to Proclus and Porphyry.[10]

Raine's method was criticized by the foremost university critic of his day, F. R. Leavis.[11] Leavis's criticism and subsequent methodology has curtailed investigation into ideas and thoughts that are esoteric. This present work is an attempt to redress the balance, drawing upon several disciplines, particularly literature and philosophy. While I am concerned with an understanding of Homeric and other Greek texts in the light of Blake's vision of the sexes, I draw also on illustrative material from diverse cultures and traditions.

When we look at the concept of Mother Right, in its relationship with birth and death, Blake's sacred marriage appears very different. The Mother Goddess is a singular entity, sometimes believed to possess the power of parthenogenesis, a belief that separates the sexes rather than enabling their union. By ignoring the other in the advocating of matriarchy, we are in the same situation of one-sidedness as rule by patriarchy. And one of our earliest examples of this type of patriarchy is Homer's *Iliad*. While it is true that the female goddesses employ many means to achieve their ends—and, in the case of Hera, quite successfully at times—nevertheless the plight of the mortal woman depicted here is a sorry one. For anything better we need to look at the *Odyssey,*

[10] Roger Sworder, *Science and Religion in Archaic Greece,* 2008, San Rafael, CA, Sophia Perennis, 292.

[11] Sworder, ibid.

where the emphasis upon marriage and the roles of male and female are very different. Blake's emphasis on pity as a deciding attribute in the relationship between male and female is rarely shown in pre-history and Homeric works. When it is shown, predominantly it is by the gods and not by the humans.

Following on from the *Iliad* and *Odyssey*, Greek thought flourishes and appears to diverge from these epics. We are able, however, to discern traces of paternalistic or maternalistic notions in even the most diehard adherent of either strain of thought. Some of the major thinkers from that period; Hesiod, Aristotle, Aeschylus, Aristotle, Parmenides, Plato, and in the *Homerica* "The Hymn to Demeter" follow one or other of these lines of thought. Knowledge of Greek philosophy has an influence upon the monotheistic religions, and the divergent strains of Greek thought are reflected in the esoterica and exoterica of these religions.

This study uses the female and male paradigm in Blake's work and sets it against what we know of ancient thought. In Blake's schema, female and male, soul and spirit, are united by the act of sacred marriage, *hieros gamos*. Pity, as piety, is what enables the union of female and male to take place. When pity is functioning in its correct manner it is possible to recognize the self in the other and in so doing reach the state of Beulah named by Blake, where "Contrarieties are equally True."

PART ONE

William Blake

1

William Blake and Pity

WILLIAM BLAKE'S position in history, on the cusp of the Industrial Revolution, and his recognition of the great losses suffered by English men and women after the Enclosure movement, caused him to write in response.[1] This is undeniable. Other writers and thinkers also wrote in response to society's upheaval—from More, with his man-eating sheep,[2] to Kingsley's tale of the chimney sweeps.[3] Dickens, Wollstonecraft, Marx, and various writers in between, all attacked the problems that most troubled them. Although Blake responds to the physical markers in history and in his own surroundings, and sees these physical losses clearly, he is more concerned with the greater loss of spiritual cohesiveness. Blake's enormous breadth of traditional knowledge allows him to show us what the loss of time-honored wisdom had brought. His very keen distress at the spiritual condition of his beloved Albion allows a pre-rationalized world to emerge. Nevertheless, his work was largely unknown in his lifetime and, indeed, forgotten until Ellis and Yeats brought Blake back into

---

[1] William Blake (1757–1827). Blake's memorial in Westminster Abbey is as follows: "Poet, Artist, Mystic."

[2] Sir Thomas More, *More's Utopia and a Dialogue of Comfort,* trans. Robinson, 1957, London, J. M. Dent, 26:

> Forsooth, my lord, quoth I, your sheep that were wont to be so meek and tame and so small eaters, now, as I hear say, be become so great devourers and so wild that they eat up, and swallow down, the very men themselves. They consume, destroy, and devour whole fields, houses, and cities.

[3] Charles Kingsley (1819–1875), Clergyman and novelist. *Water Babies* is now read as a children's book, although it was written in defence of the "climbing boys."

the literature of England, in 1893, almost seventy years after his death.[4] Since that publication there have been many conflicting ideas concerning his beliefs.

I have little doubt that Blake was a Christian, even though he was not a conventional observer.[5] Again, this is an area where many have attempted to fit his beliefs into more rigid schemata. J. P. Thompson, in the book written before he died, sets out to prove that Blake was a Muggletonian.[6] His first biographer, Alexander Gilchrist,[7] queried Blake's Gnostic beliefs. But Blake's belief in the link between pity and Christianity is consistently shown throughout his work, starting with the early engraved books he produced at home. Blake illustrates pity in "The Divine Image" and "The Human Abstract":

> For Mercy, Pity, Peace and Love
> Is God, our Father dear.[8]

contrasted with:

> Pity would be no more
> If we did not make somebody poor...
> And mutual fear brings peace
> Till the selfish loves increase.[9]

In "The Divine Image" Blake is using pity as one of the divine

---

[4] Edwin John Ellis & William Butler Yeats, *The Works of William Blake*, 1893, London, Bernard Quaritch.

[5] Kathleen Raine, *Blake and Tradition*, 2 vols., 1968, Princeton, Princeton University Press. One of the greatest writers concerning Blake and his traditional values was Kathleen Raine and it is her work that motivates this essay.

[6] E. P. Thompson, *Witness Against the Beast: William Blake and the Moral Law*, 1993, Cambridge, Cambridge University Press. Thompson was a Marxist historian who had used Blake's comments to ratify his own position regarding the horrors of industrialization. His last book was an attempt to understand Blake's complex beliefs.

[7] Alexander Gilchrist, *Life of William Blake*, 1942, London, J. M. Dent & Sons.

[8] *Blake: Complete Writings*, ed. Keynes, 1989, Oxford, Oxford University Press, K. 117, SOI.DI:5. All quotations from Blake will use the Keynes edition of his work: thus "K" followed by title, book or page number, and line numbers.

[9] K. 217, SOE.HA:1–2, 5–6.

attributes.[10] When the divine within us pities the divine in another, this is a union as opposed to the divisiveness of the pity shown in "The Human Abstract." In this poem the separation from our self and another's self allows a distancing to occur from the other's suffering.

The England of Blake's lifetime paid little heed to the true meaning of pity. In Cobbett's view, "the chain of connection between the rich and the poor,"[11] which had been present before industrialization, was being tested to its breaking-point. It is my belief that this particular connection had been tested far earlier than the Industrial Revolution and the time when Cobbett was writing. One can see the disconnection as far back as the Enclosure Movements, centuries before the additional stress of industrialization. The modern connotation of the word "pity" implies a feeling projected down toward someone weaker, or more unfortunate, than the pitier. This places both in an invidious position. Modern pity is false to its original etymological root within the English language. Unlike piety—that is, true pity—becomes an act of condescension and not a meeting of equals engaged in an act of service to the divine. This is the false pity described by Blake in "The Human Abstract." This is also our modern pity.

For Blake, abstraction from the divine in man began with Francis Bacon (1561–1626). Seen as the founder of modern empirical science, Bacon stressed the principle of proof. When the principle of proof is applied to religion, doubt can then erode the virtue of faith. In Blakean terminology, doubt is a negation,

> He who replies to words of Doubt
> Doth put the Light of Knowledge out.[12]

---

[10] The Oxford Dictionary of Etymology, ed: C.T. Onions, et al., 1982, Oxford, Clarendon Press, s.v:

"pity" † clemency, mercy: compassion XIII: † piety XIV... L. *pietāt-tās* PIETY. In later L. *pietàs*, prop. dutifulness, gratitude; acquired the sense of compassion, kindness; O.F. *pité* and *pieté* had both senses, but were subsequently differentiated, and this was reflected in the corr. English forms as now used. Hence pity vb. XVI (More) perh. after F. pitiable XV, pitiful XIV, pitiless XV (Hoccleve).

[11] Asa Briggs and John Saville, Eds: *Essays in Labour History*, 1967, London, MacMillan, 45.

[12] *K.* 433, AUG:95.

The knowledge referred to by Blake is not gained by empirical observation of material objects but is the true intelligence of the divine. Sir Isaac Newton (1642–1727), whose discoveries defined the material universe, was justly recognized as an extraordinary thinker even by Blake. Blake's disagreement with Newton was the latter's apparent acceptance of empiricism and measurement as the only means of gaining knowledge. The third member of the triumvirate was John Locke, [1632-1704]. Locke's proposal that reason was the prime power of man effectively denied any other source of knowledge except that gained by the use of the five senses and man's rational ability. Blake dismissed Locke's premise with this argument:

> I. Man's perceptions are not bounded by organs of perception; he perceives more than sense (tho' ever so acute) can discover.
> II. Reason, or the ratio of all we have already known, is not the same that it shall be when we know more…
> VII. The desire of Man being Infinite, the possession is Infinite & himself Infinite.[13]

In direct contrast to the limiting of man's powers to just that which is accessible to his senses, Blake saw knowledge as innate, obtained only by inner vision, the "Divine Imagination."

When Blake caricatures this trio of rationalists, speaking as the voice of reason,

> I am God, O Sons of Men! I am your Rational Power!
> Am I not Bacon & Newton & Locke who teach Humility to Man,
> Who teach Doubt & Experiment?[14]

he does so because he sees that these three men of reason have tied man to the Material Universe.

> No more could they rise at will
> In the Infinite void, but bound down
> To earth by their narrowing perceptions
> They lived a period of years;

---

[13] K.97, TNN:1.
[14] K.685, J. 54:16.

Then left a noisome body
To the jaws of devouring darkness.[15]

Mankind is degraded to the position of seeking to satisfy illusory material wants, while ostensibly elevated to a position of supremacy in a society governed by reason. True freedom is unattainable when man's reason is the measure of his worth. This is always a denial of the divinity within him precisely because divinity cannot be enumerated or tabulated. It is that which is infinite, while still being centered within the individual, for,

> . . . as in your own Bosom you bear your Heaven
> And Earth & all you behold; tho' it appears Without, it is Within,
> In your Imagination, of which this World of Mortality is but a Shadow.[16]

If "the doors of our perception were cleansed,"[17] we would have the ability to recognize "the unwavering heart of well-rounded truth,"[18] Coleridge's "common centre," the "hallow'd centre" of Blake within ourselves. The search for that recognition is an exercise of Intellect, not Reason.

As Blake points out, this recognition or union allows pity to function in its true manner, which is as a facet of God. By limiting our perceptions of ourselves and therefore of the greater universe, Reason also divides pity from its divine source. Thus pity becomes an abstract emotion extended to others; not a recognition of us in them, but a duty to be performed. The performance of this duty, moreover, becomes an act of withdrawal from the person being pitied, and an act of withdrawal from the divine within the pitier.

The creation of a lay bureaucracy to administer the distribution of social pity is a further withdrawal from its divine source, the divinity in man. This pity, the need for which has been created

[15] K. 236, UR. IX:45.

[16] K. 709, J. 71:17.

[17] K. 15, MHH. 14:12.

[18] Parmenides, *Early Greek Philosophy*, trans. Jonathan Barnes, 1987, Middlesex, Penguin Classics, 131. This is the most obtainable work but its commentary is unsatisfactory.

by a rational society, is transferred to bodies governed by the principles of reason. Reasonable men, who are more likely to be ruled by the necessity to present an economic return on the money spent, administer this "social pity" on an abstract basis. Pity, true piety, becomes an incidental and individual occurrence. The problem of the poor has always been present, but with the Enclosure movements, which began in the reign of Henry VII (1485–1509), the poor became "something," rather than "someone."

Successive Tudor monarchs attempted to redress this problem with varying degrees of success. The commencement of the Enclosure Movement eventually led to the end of the reciprocity of dues between the three major levels of society and saw the start of the rationalization process to which is tied the material worth of any deed. And how does Blake see this? In *Songs of Innocence* he writes the poem "The Ecchoing Green."

> Till the little ones, weary,
> No more can be merry;
> The sun does descend,
> And our sports have an end.
> Round the laps of their mothers
> Many sisters and brothers,
> Like birds in their nest,
> Are ready for rest,
> And sport no more seen
> On the darkening Green.[19]

The echoing Green is the world of rural England before the Enclosure movements removed these aspects of life and leisure. Children, sisters and brothers, playing as children should, until finally at rest on their mothers' knees. But in *Songs of Experience* he paints a much sadder picture.

> Then come home, my children, the sun is gone down,
> And the dews of the night arise;
> Your spring & your day are wasted in play,
> And your winter and night in disguise.[20]

[19] K.116, SOI. EG: 21.
[20] K.212, SOE. NS: 5.

No longer are children to waste their days in play and their carer is no longer a parent but an abstract figure, the Nurse. The plight of poor children in Blake's lifetime was dire, and he responded to this with many poems in these early published works.

But the necessity for Poor Laws, our earliest, State administered "social pity," occurred at the time of separation from the Universal Church.[21] It is unreasonable to assume that men of piety did not exist within either the separated Church or the many sects which follow that separation. Nevertheless, this division coincides with the necessity for institutionalized pity. During the period of Blake's writing and England's industrialization, various proposals were made regarding the problem of the poor. But the particular point of separation within the Church and man that was a consequence of the Tudor rule is of importance. The division created by Henry VIII and the new learning disseminated with the Renaissance created a belief in the individual that replaced the ideal of God in man. As an individual, a mere monarch, Henry had established a national Church—and far from suffering, the nation as a whole had prospered since its withdrawal from the Holy Roman Church. And the history of the Christian religion within England is a history of further fragmentation. Attempting to assess the relative spirituality of Catholic, or the new "Anglican," Puritan, Muggletonian, or any of the many sects that develop from then on, is useless. The danger point is reached when an individual, without ordination or formal training, is placed as spiritual head of a Church by virtue of being a nation's temporal head. Guénon claims that

> individualism [is] the denial of any principle superior to the individuality and, as a consequence, the reduction of civilization in all its departments to purely human elements.[22]

---

[21] Brian Inglis, *Poverty and The Industrial Revolution*, 1972, London, Panther Books, 43:

In 1531 the State intervened, taking the first tentative step towards a national poor law. Five years later, another Act had to be passed, its preamble almost shamefacedly admitting that its predecessor had made provision neither for finding work . . . nor for raising funds to provide it.

[22] René Guénon, *Crisis of the Modern World*, 1975, London, Luzac & Co., 51.

An act by an individual, which resulted in the separation of the Church of England from the Church of Rome, as well as the closure of the monasteries, invoked the following divisive events. The Church was no longer in the same position of carer for the sick and needy within that society. The necessity arose for social legislation to control and alleviate the problem. Marx describes the situation,[23] and while not advocating a return to pre-Reformation England, he is acknowledging the schism that was, and still remains, apparent between those who possess property and those who do not.[24] Beginning with the Enclosure Movement, the breakdown between the differing groups was finalized by the time of the Restoration. So devastating was this that Marx com-

[23] Karl Marx, *Capital*, ed: Friedrich Engels, 1952, Chicago, Encyclopaedia Britannica, 358:

The process of forcible expropriation of the people received in the sixteenth century a new and frightful impulse from the Reformation, and from the consequent colossal spoliation of the church property. The Catholic Church was, at the time of the Reformation, feudal proprietor of a great part of the English land. The suppression of the monasteries, etc., hurled their inmates into the proletariat. The estates of the church were to a large extent given away to rapacious royal favourites, or sold at a nominal price to speculating farmers and citizens, who drove out, *en masse*, the hereditary sub-tenants and threw their holdings into one. The legally guaranteed property of the poorer folk in a part of the church's tithes was tacitly confiscated. *"Pauper ubique jacet,"* cried Queen Elizabeth, after a journey through England. In the forty-third year of her reign, the nation was obliged to recognize pauperism officially by the introduction of a poor rate. By 16 of Charles I, 4, it was declared perpetual, and in fact only in 1834 did it take a new and harsher form. These immediate results of the Reformation were not its most lasting ones. The property of the church formed the religious bulwark of the traditional conditions of landed property. With its fall, these were no longer tenable.

[24] Marx, ibid., 359:

After the restoration of the Stuarts, the landed proprietors carried, by legal means, an act of usurpation, effected everywhere on the continent without any legal formality. They abolished the feudal tenure of land, i.e., they got rid of all its obligations to the State, "indemnified" the State by taxes on the peasantry and the rest of the mass of the people, vindicated for themselves the rights of modern private property in estates to which they had only a feudal title, and, finally, passed those laws of settlement, which, mutatis mutandis, had the same effect on the English agricultural labourer as the edict of the Tartar Boris Godunof on the Russian peasantry.

pared the result to the serfdom which existed in 16th-century Russia. That oppressive form of serfdom existed in Russia but a less
well recognized form was functioning in England.

The division or splintering of various religious groups, though
motivated by the search for spiritual fulfillment, resulted in the
practice of religion being no longer national, let alone universal.
The recognition of its own power by Parliament, and the gradual
erosion of the monarch's power, may be traced to this period of
time. With the act of "43rd Elizabeth,"[25] compulsory contribu-
tions assessed by Justices of the Peace abstracted pity from its
divine source and commenced the progress towards the modern
interpretation of the word and the act.

Blake's lifetime saw these divisions become even more apparent. The country was governed by the Parliament, itself not yet
democratically elected, but representative of the landed interest.
The result of this was further divisions within the society, which
could not be healed by the Government's social legislation. Eighteenth Squirocracy across England stole the common lands. The
Squires were the problem, not the solution. The national Church
was governed by men from the upper levels of that society, many
of whom saw their position as a profession and not as a spiritual
calling, and who were: "suffocating in an Eighteenth-Century
torpor, with arid moralizing predominating."[26] The increased
enclosures, all capable of rational explanation but tremendously
destructive of a traditional way of life, were rapidly demolishing
access to common land. For anyone capable of recognizing the
divine in another, this was a cause for sorrow. The systems
employed to achieve better yields from the land paid little heed
to the human harvesters, many of whom were forced to seek
employment in mills, factories, and mines or simply to starve.
Concern was shown for the more unfortunate members of this
society by many who were genuinely moved by their plight, but
predominantly the enlightened self-interest of those in power

[25] Inglis, op. cit., 44.
[26] Louis Cazamian, *The Social Novel in England* 1830–1850, 1973, London,
Routledge & Kegan Paul, 33.

meant that "facile pity was the characteristic of England and France alike in the late Eighteenth Century."[27]

For Blake, the church was governed not by spirituality but by reason. Under the governorship of reason, moral law had replaced the spiritual.

> Throughout the century the sermons of Anglican preachers, whatever their party, though most markedly among the Whigs, kept the miraculous character of Christianity as far as possible in the background.[28]

This was the position within England and the national church—reason governed by moralistic law. Unrepresented as they were, and still are, the poor, the weak, and defenceless stood little chance when pitted against the voices of reason.

Many authors and poets attempted to address the problems raised by this moralistic, rational governance. One of the most well known and influential was Charles Dickens. The questions asked by Blake and Dickens demonstrate their differences. Dickens asks, "What can be done to ease the suffering?" and the remedy proposed is not unlike the application of a sticking plaster to a broken leg. Blake asks, "Why is it so?" and proposes a complete reversal of society's attitudes to achieve his aims. The "sticking plaster" remedy was the pattern for social legislation then and now. Pragmatic realism as opposed to ethical mysticism were the

> two intellectual movements . . . never systematically combined: they mingled confusedly. . . . England found the formula for internal stability in the rejection of any formula whatsoever.[29]

Other writers supported Blake's stance against the abstraction of man from the divine. Mrs Barbauld, writing in 1874, says: "Respect in the infant the future man. Destroy not in the man the

[27] Cazamian, op. cit., 78.
[28] Elie Halevy, *A History of the People in 1815*, 1987, London, Routledge & Kegan Paul, 343.
[29] Cazamian, op. cit., 300.

rudiments of an angel."[30] As the Ancient Greeks extended their hospitality to any stranger, thus guarding against insulting a god, so St Paul instructed the Hebrews, "Be not forgetful to entertain strangers: for thereby some have entertained angels unawares" Heb. 13:2. And Blake: "Then cherish pity, lest you drive an angel from your door."[31] This is Blake's piety, which is a divine act, and not the false pity, which becomes "a devouring flame,"

> Thought chang'd the infinite to a serpent, that
> which pitieth
> To a devouring flame.[32]

This pity not only devours those it pities but also the pitier. The inability to recognize the divine within the other has as its corollary non-recognition of the divine within oneself. When pity is governed by reason, it is relatively easy to forget that one's fellow man is being dealt with. Men who would no doubt wince if they saw a person they were familiar with being physically hurt have no problem refusing to pass legislation that would benefit those at the bottom of the heap. Social pity allows this to happen without any discomfort whatsoever because it is abstracted from humanity and its divinity. The social novelists' greatest contribution was the familiarization of the larger world with the problems of "the Poor," allowing some recognition of their fellow man to take place. For some with charitable souls, there was a reaction. Nevertheless. often it was still an act of condescension towards others, an abstraction that had to be addressed in the most economical way.

The history of England's Poor Laws makes sorry reading. By the process of abstraction, Cobbett's "Scotch feelosofers," Blake's practitioners of "Abstract Philosophy," drew away from their fellow man's suffering. Building upon Adam Smith's policy of *laissez-faire*, the English Parliament constructed their *laissez-nous faire* system. In effect, this meant that they would only intercede when

[30] David V. Erdman, *Blake: Prophet against Empire*, 1977, Princeton, Princeton University Press, 125. Quoting: Grace A. Oliver, *Life of Mrs.Barbauld*, 98.
[31] K. 122, SOI. HT:12.
[32] K. 241, EUR. 10:16.

intercession would aid the ruling classes, or when forced to do so "in the teeth of indifference and greed."[33] By withdrawing from the concept of regarding the poor as their fellow man, Parliament more easily regarded the poor as a problem that required a solution, no matter how temporary that solution might prove to be. But by failing to recognize what was, for Blake, self-evident, they were able to forget that they too shared in:

> ...the Eternal Vision, the Divine Similitude,
> In loves and tears of brothers, sisters, sons, fathers and friends,
> Which if Man ceases to behold, he ceases to exist.[34]

When guided only by reason, man's dealings with his fellow man are negated by abstraction. This withdrawal allows contemplation of another's suffering to be, at best, uncaring and, at worst, actively callous. Events such as the total destruction of an entire city by a single explosive device, or the death of one small boy trapped in a chimney, suffocating and, eventually, incinerated, are all able to be rationally justified. There is always a valid reason (usually economic) why corrective measures cannot be taken. The rise of individuality had paradoxically led to a fall in the value of a single human life. Confined by the material, generated world, the individual: "enter[s] the merciless battle of each against all for life,"[35] and is imprisoned. When reason is able to justify the elimination of, or despair for, one human life, then Love, Pity, and Charity are false pretenders to their names. If we disregard the infinite and accept reason's material assessment as our only test of an individual's worth, then in the words of Urizen—the Zoa who represents man's reasoning powers—we have accepted:

> that Human Form
> You call Divine is but a Worm seventy inches long
> That creeps forth in a night & is dried in the morning sun,

---

[33] Cazamian, op. cit., 29.
[34] K. 664, J. 38:11.
[35] Cazamian, op. cit., 16.

In fortuitous concourse of memorys accumulated & lost.
It plows the Earth in its own conceit.[36]

For Blake it is the Negation that must be continually fought against.

There is a Negation, & there is a Contrary:
The Negation must be destroy'd to redeem the Contraries.
The Negation is the Spectre, the Reasoning Power in Man:
This is a false Body, an Incrustation over my Immortal
Spirit, A Selfhood which must be put off & annihilated
alway.[37]

Nowhere else in Blake's work does he state so clearly—and he does so many times—just what the end of man is if he is governed only by reason. The end product is a spectre of a man. An empty husk whose immortal spirit has been destroyed, a selfhood wherein "to think for oneself is always to think of oneself."[38] For "In Selfhood, we are nothing, but fade away in morning's breath"[39]

Blake's responses to what were immediate social evils, occurring at a particular moment in the world's history, transcend that moment. It may be that that "moment" induced a particular response and emphasis because man's ability to rationalize, to reason, had allowed degradation of his fellow man to reach endemic proportions. But this method of governance has continued to the present day. The operative mode of today's society is false pity, legislated for by a temporal authority,

Till pity is become a trade, and generosity a science
That men get rich by,[40]

and it is difficult not to imagine Blake viewing our modern world with dismay.

[36] K. 659, J. 33:4.
[37] K. 533, M. 40:32.
[38] Ananda K. Coomaraswamy, *Christian and Oriental Philosophy of Art*, 1956 New York, Dover, 38.
[39] K. 675, J. 45:13.
[40] K. 200, AM. 11:10.

Blake, engraved "The First Book of Urizen" in 1794. The following year saw the commencement of his unfinished prophetic work, "Vala, and The Four Zoas," on which he worked for nine years.[41] In this work Blake makes very powerful use of pity in both senses of the word. Societal pity is demonstrated by Urizen, who represents man's reasoning power, as he prescribes and proscribes from his brass book of sociology. Much as a politician may do, Urizen, as god of this material world, directs his daughters on how to govern society by saying one thing and doing another:

> Listen, O Daughters, to my voice. Listen to the Words of Wisdom,
> So shall [you] govern over all; let Moral Duty tune your tongue...
> Compell the poor to live upon a Crust of bread, by soft mild arts.
> Smile when they frown, frown when they smile; & when a man looks pale
> With labor & abstinence, say he looks healthy & happy;
> And when his children sicken, let them die; there are enough
> Born, even too many, & our Earth will be overrun
> Without these arts.[42]

Now we call this "spin." Social law as laid down by Urizen enforces the division between male and female, poor and rich, and—more importantly for Blake—man and his God. The choice of a brass book in which to record these social laws echoes Paul's Epistle to the Corinthians: "Though I speak with the

[41] Blake did not engrave "Vala and The Four Zoas" but an attempt to reproduce this poem in its entirety has been made by Cettina Tramontano Magno & David Erdman, in *The Four Zoas by William Blake*, 1987, Cranbury, NJ, Associated University Presses. Magno and Erdman have included the etchings Blake had interposed loosely within the poem. These were primarily superfluous etchings from other work. I disagree with the commentary because it does not seem to engage with the poem. The interpretation attached to the sketches seems to be based upon a very physical understanding of what is a very difficult poem but which is also a deeply spiritual one. Therefore the interpretation appears superficial to this reader.

[42] K. 323, FZ. 7:110.

tongues of men and angels, and have not charity, I am become as sounding brass." 1 Cor. 13:1 This is the world of Blake's England, the beginnings of the science of economics and the precursor to our modern system of social pity.

Consistently throughout his working life Blake emphasized the acceptance of contrary states of being, and he demonstrated this most clearly with the roles of the feminine and the masculine. But he saw, in his England, the separation and withdrawal of the "haves" from the "have-nots," not as contrariety but as negation. The non-recognition of the divine within one's self allowed for treatment of another to be an abstraction. The other became a problem that might be solved by rational and reasoned arguments, a process that weighed the material worth to that society of any one person in order to assess the benefit that might be gained, and whether or not assistance could be granted to those who needed it. Man no longer looked upon his fellow man as a brother. Instead, he was an individual entering "that merciless battle of each against all" that imprisoned him in his selfhood—a selfhood which was for Blake an "incrustation over his immortal soul."

When the self becomes the measure for all things, then pity has lost its original connotation. It is no longer an act of piety extended to an other as if it were one's self, but a measuring-out of pity, for "there are enough born even too many."

> Can I see another's woe,
> And not be in sorrow too?[43]

---

[43] *K.* 122, *SOI. OAS*:1–2.

2

Blake and the Feminine

STUDYING the historical prompts to which Blake responded is one method of investigation, but it is also necessary to discuss what is more difficult in his work. Blake's mysticism provoked scorn from many of his contemporaries, and often boredom from modern critics. When the author of the Hermetic treatise *Asclepius* wrote the following words, he was anticipating what was likely to happen in his society:

> They will prefer shadows to light, and they will find death more expedient than life. No one will look up to heaven. The reverent will be thought mad, the irreverent wise; the lunatic will be thought brave, and the scoundrel will be taken for a decent person. Soul and all teachings about soul (that soul began as immortal or else expects to attain immortality) as I revealed them to you will be considered not simply laughable but even illusory. But—believe me— whoever dedicates himself to reverence of mind will find himself facing a capital penalty. They will establish new laws, new justice. Nothing holy, nothing reverent nor worthy of heaven or heavenly beings will be heard of or believed in the mind.[1]

Asclepius' words are pertinent today. The truth contained in them is borne out by the reaction of most critics to the work of William Blake. Dr Philippe Berger was a critic who at least attempted to understand Blake's mysticism, but even he found it

---

[1] *Asclepius* iii.25; *Hermetica: The Greek Corpus Hermeticum and the Latin Asclepius*, trans. Brian P. Copenhaver, 2000, Cambridge: Cambridge University Press, 82.

impossible to read Blake's work because "his mysticism is such that our language is no more sufficient to describe his visions than his pencil was capable of expressing them fully."[2]

If a compassionate critic such as Berger feels this way, then we have indeed reached the position described by Asclepius. Most contemporary critics ignore this aspect of Blake's work altogether and choose to focus upon the social, political, economic, or other material causes they feel able to distinguish within his work. This is a reductive process when applied to William Blake. To acknowledge a spiritual point of view may be difficult for literary critics. Berger and countless others have adopted what Blake would call a Urizenic view of his work and thus denied to him that level of spiritual understanding which he valued above all else. Berger does acknowledge that the "foundation of Blake's theories, as well as his art, is his mysticism";[3] but this is not praise from Berger's viewpoint, but criticism. Criticism, that is, from a literary point of view.

> Incoherencies, repetitions, breaks in the continuity of the narrative—all these would be quite enough, even if the language were clear and simple, to render much of Blake's work incomprehensible at first sight.[4]

Such inaccessibility prevents a reader or critic from achieving certainty of understanding. It allows too many variant understandings to occur. This does not fit well with someone who pursues life in a rationalist, reasoning manner, as we might assume Berger to do. It is also likely that Blake would see Berger as a "Real Enemy":

> There is no Medium or Middle state; & if a Man is the Enemy of my Spiritual Life while he pretends to be the Friend of my Corporeal, he is a Real Enemy—but the Man may be the friend of my Spiritual Life while he seems the Enemy of my Corporeal, but Not Vice Versa.[5]

---

[2] Philippe Berger, *William Blake: Poet and Mystic,* trans. Conner, 1915, New York, E. P. Dutton, 20.

[3] Ibid., 68.

[4] Ibid., 219.

[5] K. 822.

The corporeal life, which in Blake's mythology is governed by Reason—named Urizen—is quite secondary when compared with the life of the spirit. To deny this spiritual reading of Blake's work—to focus merely upon the quite obvious prompts from the society that surrounded him or to attempt to place him within a literary school, discarding what does not fit—is to become a "Real Enemy" of Blake and of what he found to be of prime importance. The spiritual impetus behind Blake's work was so central that he saw himself merely as a conduit. We do have proof, in his own words, that Blake believed himself to be in direct contact with a metaphysical reality that was the driving force behind all his writings.[6] These writings are inspired in the traditional meaning of the word, that is, Spirit is infused into them. Blake's metaphysical reality was consistently present for his entire working career, but particularly so in his unfinished prophetic work *The Four Zoas*. This poem depicts a Christian metaphysical reality that may have been peculiar to Blake, but is undeniably present in this work. This reality is also present in a more refined manner in both *Milton* and *Jerusalem*, the other two large and completed prophetic works. It is also possible to see his belief in the idea of a spiritual life, on this earth and hereafter, in his earlier pieces.

Blake's argument in *There is No Natural Religion* (First and Second Series, c. 1788), addresses the idea that we are caught in "mind-forged manacles" if we rely only upon our senses as the primary source for knowledge—that is, knowledge of the infinite. In the First Series, the argument is: "Man has no notion of moral fitness but from Education. Naturally he is only a natural organ subject to Sense." Blake answers that argument in the Second Series: "Man's perceptions are not bounded by organs of perception; he perceives more than sense (tho' ever so acute) can discover." The concluding argument in the Second Series indi-

---

[6] See Blake's letters to Dr Trusler (*K.* 791, *K.* 793), to William Hayley (*K.* 797), and to Thomas Butts (*K.* 812, *K.* 823). These are but a few of the references which Blake himself makes to his being inspired, "without Premeditation & even against my Will."

cates clearly that Blake's emphasis was continuously upon the spiritual.

> *VII.* The desire of Man being Infinite, the possession is Infinite & himself Infinite.
> *Application.* He who sees the Infinite in all things, sees God. He who sees the Ratio only, sees himself only.
> Therefore God becomes as we are, that we may be as he is.[7]

The Marriage of Heaven and Hell was engraved between one and four years later. In this poem Blake reiterates his position *vis-à-vis* the importance of the soul, and yet appears to alter his position on the role of the five senses:

> Man has no Body distinct from his Soul; for that call'd Body is a portion of Soul discern'd by the five Senses, the chief inlets of Soul in this age.[8]

We must remember that the body is a mutable part of the human composite, the Soul, which also contains the immutable part, the Spirit. The Christian and, indeed, Platonic, denial of the importance of the senses, the body, the physical self as the means to the spirit, was not Blake's path.[9]

But Blake appears to counter even this position further on in *The Marriage of Heaven and Hell* when he returns from his sojourn with the angels and devils.

> When I came home: on the abyss of the five senses, where a flat sided steep frowns over the present world, I saw a mighty Devil folded in black clouds, hovering on the sides of the rock: with corroding fires he wrote the following sentence now perceived by the minds of men, & read by them on earth:
> How do you know but ev'ry Bird that cuts the airy way,

---

[7] *K.*97–98,*TNN.*

[8] *K.*149, *MHH.*4:1.

[9] I refer the reader to Kathleen Raine's *Blake and Tradition*, 2 vols., 1968, Princeton, Princeton University Press. Raine demonstrates clearly the influence of neo-Platonism on Blake's thought. [See 104, refs 19, 21, 22, and 117, refs 48, 49.]

Is an immense world of delight, clos'd by your senses five?[10]

Blake distinguishes the five senses as an abyss, the world cave, but he does not deny the use of these senses. What he sees with the eye of the imagination—the faculty he prized above all others—is himself in the normal world as a devilish form engraving two of the most beautiful lines in English poetry. We would do well to remember, however, that the sojourn his spiritual self has just taken has been in the company of devils who are Energy and eternal delight; therefore, the devilish role his physical self displays is linked directly to the non-material world. Chatterton's lines in *The Bristowe Tragedie* may have been the source for Blake:

How dydd I know that every darte
That cutte the airie waie
Might nott fynde passage toe my harte
And close myne eyes for aie.[11]

Chatterton's quatrain is dispirited, sad, melancholic. Blake gives us a vision of delight that is closed from our "senses five," while Chatterton only promises a finite end. While Blake's poetry does address the sorrows and pain of the material world, there is always joy to be found in his work. His earlier poetry appears to be deceptively simple, as may be seen in the earliest inscribed works *The Songs of Innocence* and *The Songs of Experience*—particularly when compared with the larger, prophetic works. The dates given for these by Geoffrey Keynes are 1789–94, with *The Book of Thel* written in 1789. Blake's sources, whether social or philosophical, are not the only key to understanding his work. It is far more likely that Blake, working as he did on *The Four Zoas* between 1795–1804, assimilated all that occurred in his immediate world: the French Revolution, proto-industrialization, displacement of

---

[10] *K.*150, *MHH.*6–7:7–13.

[11] "The Bristowe Tragedie," lines 133–136; *The Complete Works of Thomas Chatterton*, eds. Taylor & Hoover, 2 vols., 1971, Oxford, Oxford University Press, i., 11. According to S. Foster Damon, Blake owned a copy of Chatterton's poems but did not annotate it. *A Blake Dictionary*, 1973, London, Thames and Hudson, 78.

farming communities, the use of children in manufactories and mines, enslavement at home and abroad, as well as Gnostic, Swedenborgian, Jewish, and particular Christian symbols to create his own mythology. The relationship between the macrocosmic Spirit and the Soul is epitomized by Blake in the microcosmic male and the female; this is a recurrent theme used by Blake throughout his entire career. Relating the macrocosm to the microcosm is a very powerful and traditional technique. Blake uses this technique to demonstrate the manner in which society and humanity were sickening.

The *Visions of the Daughters of Albion* is where Blake created one of his most powerful feminine characters. The hero Oothoon, despite her sufferings, is the strongest and most spiritually centered of the three protagonists.[12] Oothoon is raped by Bromion and rejected by Theotormon, whom she loves, and then trapped in a loveless marriage with Bromion. The opening stanzas of the poem deal with slavery in America and proceed to enslavement within marriage, personified by Oothoon. It seems apparent that *Visions of The Daughters of Albion* was written in response to Mary Wollstonecraft's *Vindication of the Rights of Women*.[13] But Blake was not content with Wollstonecraft's praiseworthy aim to make women's material position equal to that of men. It was not enough for him for woman to be given voting power in the political sphere; to be allowed the chance for education and choice in career; and to have a recognition of rights within marriage, both in the choices of partners and the conduct of the marriage itself. Oothoon's ability to find the inviolable center within herself

[12] My use of "hero" as an appellation for both Oothoon and Enitharmon is deliberate. My impression is that "heroine" has the connotation of passivity. Oothoon and Enitharmon demonstrate and are the means by which the spiritual dimension is shown, and are, consequently, active. Oothoon achieves a spiritual peace that is not shared by her two male counterparts. Enitharmon is the means by which the final resolution is achieved in *The Four Zoas*. Why does Blake choose to do this? I think he is ensuring the recognition of these strengths which he designates as female. It is the same strength Homer allows Odysseus, in the figure of Athene, after his rebirth from the sea; therefore they are all three heroes.

[13] Raine, *Blake and Tradition*, op. cit., i.,70.

allows Blake to present a most marvellous hero. Of the trio, she is the only one who achieves this transcendence that removes her from earthly pain. What Blake chooses to do for women is different from the path followed by Wollstonecraft. His hero, Oothoon, surpasses her masculine counterparts and achieves what should be the ultimate aim of all humanity if we did not consider teachings regarding the soul as "not simply laughable but even illusory."

In 1915, Berger wrote that in "Blake's eyes, woman was always an inferior being."[14] Anne Mellor, writing in 1988, states that Blake was one of "the canon of six poets" who upheld a traditional view of women that placed them quite low in society.[15] These statements by critics from opposing sexes espousing different literary positions and spanning seventy-odd years, are indicative of a generally held position. But they are misreadings of Blake's poetry, if not of his intentions. In answer to this common misconception, I would argue that far from lowering the role of women, Blake placed the feminine not in a pre-eminent position, but in a position of equality with the masculine. Christianity has not always been so even-handed. As Frithjof Schuon says:

> Christian theology . . . has been led to evaluate the feminine sex with a maximum of pessimism. According to some, it is man alone and not woman who was made in the image of God, whereas the Bible affirms, not only that God created man in His image, but also that "male and female created He them," which has been misinterpreted with much ingenuity.[16]

In particular, Blake allocates the attribute of pity to woman as the means by which spiritual fulfillment or transcendence of the mortal state can be achieved. This is a traditional view of woman and man that duplicates the roles of the soul and the spirit. Mellor's statement that a traditional view of woman necessarily

[14] Berger, op. cit., 26.

[15] Anne K. Mellor, ed., *Romanticism and Feminism*, 1988, Indianapolis: Indiana University Press, 8.

[16] Frithjof Schuon, *Esoterism As Principle and as Way*, trans. Stoddart, 1990, Bedfont, Middlesex, Perennial Books, 135.

places her in a lowly position shows a very different perspective to that of Blake. Only by way of the feminine, the soul, is the spirit-intellect, the masculine, able to achieve transcendence. Error occurs where this perception is mistakenly seen to be patriarchal, or is used to patriarchal ends; when acknowledgement is not given to the idea that the soul and the spirit—represented as feminine and masculine—are both contained within each female and male. This is not a jostle for supremacy between one sex and the other. Ananda Coomaraswamy illustrates this with a quotation from the *Aitareya Aranyaka*:

> This self gives itself to that self, and that self to this self; they become one another; with the one form he (in whom the marriage has been consummated) is unified with yonder world, and with the other united to this world.[17]

This "he" is any man or woman. It is the marrying of opposites, the mutable and the immutable, the soul and the spirit, which is represented by the union of self to self, and therefore the union of self with the divine—which is the necessary path to be undertaken by female and male. This acknowledgement that "he" and "she" represent soul and spirit and are contained within each and every one, is present in the Western tradition: present, but somewhat obscured at the time of Blake's writing. The use of Blake's *The Four Zoas* to illustrate this union of soul and spirit appears to be an obvious one. Nevertheless, this unfinished work is extremely difficult to interpret. Blake gives his masculine persona, Los, the following words to speak to Enitharmon, his feminine counterpart—

> Where thou & I in undivided Essence walk'd about
> Imbodied, thou my garden of delight & I the spirit in the
>   garden;
> Mutual there we dwelt in one another's joy.[18]

—he is in one sense describing a union that existed in the material world where the couple dwelt in mutual joy, but he is also

---

[17] *Aitareya Aranyaka* 2.3–7; cited in *Coomaraswamy*, ed. Roger Lipsey, Bollingen Series LXXXIX, 3 vols., 1977, Princeton, Princeton University Press, II.32.
[18] K.327, FZ.7:271.

clearly delineating the spiritual division of soul and spirit. The "garden of delight" represents both the soul and the feminine maker of manifestation; the "spirit in the garden" is the male and the immutable part of the human composite, the spirit. Neither exists wholly without the other, and it is only recognition of this fact that enables the final subsumation, after death to the physical life, to take place. "Thou" and "I" thus represent both the male and female joyously dwelling in this material world, the garden, and spiritual divisions within each male and female of soul and spirit.

To stretch the analogy further—and much has been written on Blake's punning use of names—let us look at the names of these protagonists. Los is often regarded as an anagram for Sol, but Enitharmon is a little more complicated. She is the daughter of Tharmas and Enion. Tharmas is the ocean and Enion the generative instinct: thus he is the formless and she the formative. Enitharmon therefore represents the world itself, land and sea, "the garden of delight," while Los is the light of the world, the "spirit in the garden." This is Blake's celebration of the joy to be found in the physical union of male and female, and the spiritual union of soul and spirit.

> What is it men in women do require?
> The lineaments of Gratified Desire.
> What is it women do in men require?
> The lineaments of Gratified Desire.[19]

The idea that the union of male and female represents the greater union of humanity and its God is repeated throughout Blake's work. This message is also found in the teachings of the Jewish religion concerning sexuality within marriage.

> Like almost all the other major religions, Judaism has a complex set of laws governing human sexuality. However, in one major respect, the Jewish attitude toward sexuality is unique: it wholeheartedly approves of sex and of sexual pleasure. Not sex as an unfortunate but necessary way of

---

[19] K.180, *Poems from the Notebook*, 1793, n. 46.

continuing the species, but sex as a holy experience, a *mitz-vah*.[20]

Within the Christian tradition the attitude may be seen as more ambivalent, and it is particularly here that Blake's "mind-forged manacles" seem apparent. Not for him the Christian belief that human love and sexual gratification were somehow tainted by sin. As Schuon states:

> In a Christian atmosphere, sexuality in itself, isolated from every distorting context, readily acquires the opprobrium of "bestiality," whereas in reality nothing that is human is bestial by its nature; that is why we are men and not beasts.[21]

His point is that Western Christianity, following the "theology of Augustinian inspiration," sees only sin in sexual union, and (until baptism) in the children born of that union. Although childless in his own union, Blake did not share this point of view. Children were, to him, the "Eternal creation flowing from the Divine humanity in Jesus."[22]

The correspondence of marriage to a spiritual ascent is thus described by Coomaraswamy:

> The true union prefigured by the rite is a nuptial fusion apart from the consciousness of "I" and "thou": "As a man embraced by a darling bride is conscious neither of a 'within' nor a 'without,' so the Person embraced by the Providential-spirit knows naught of a 'within' nor a 'without.'"[23]

It is in this sense that Blake utilizes the sense of touch, the ultimate sense that enables us to transcend the mortal state. From this union with the "darling bride" may come the symbol of our immortality, the child. The child is not just the symbol of growth and plenitude, a furthering of the species, but symbolizes also

---

[20] George Robinson, *Essential Judaism: A Complete Guide to Beliefs, Customs, and Rituals,* 2000, New York: Simon & Schuster, 244.

[21] Schuon, op. cit., 130.

[22] K. 444, LJ.

[23] *Coomaraswamy,* ed. Roger Lipsey, op. cit., citing *Brhadanyaka Upanishad* 4.3.21.

transfiguration and spiritual growth. Blake uses the parent figure and figures in "The Little Girl Lost" and "The Little Girl Found," in *The Songs of Experience, The Book of Urizen*, and most definitively in *The Four Zoas.*

In *The Four Zoas* Blake chooses Enitharmon as the path to salvation, and uses the Four Zoas to represent four of the senses of humanity. The Zoa Urizen is associated with eyes or sight, Tharmas is the tongue or taste, Luvah nose or smell, and Los is the ear or hearing. The transfiguration or subsumation scene, which occurs in the final night of *The Four Zoas,* is triggered by the sense of touch, the fifth sense—which is perhaps the ultimate one, for this sense makes of the four senses the one.[24] Touch is the sense felt by the complete body, and the union between Los and Enitharmon clearly demonstrates that this is the path to recognition of the soul and spirit by means of the body.[25] When this embrace unites the male and female through the sense of pity, then the final transfiguration takes place.

> Obdurate Los felt Pity. Enitharmon told the tale
> Of Urthona. Los embrac'd the Spectre, first as a brother,
> Then as another Self.[26]

The masculine Zoas, Urthona, Tharmas, Urizen, Luvah, and the manifestation of Urthona, Los, do as most males do—that is, they pursue the active path. Their roles are active personifications of their respective attributes. Associated with that masculine principle is great activity that is not always accompanied by achievement, in Blake's eyes, in the material world. This is partic-

[24] One is reminded of Thomas' proof of faith (John 20:27): "Then he saith to Thomas, Reach hither thy finger, and behold my hands; and reach hither thy hand, and thrust it into my side: and be not faithless, but believing."

[25] This is done via the opening of Enitharmon's heart's gates. When they open, Los is able to enter and, eventually, all the Zoas return to their rightful places and reunion with the Absolute is able to take place. Cf. René Guénon, *Studies in Hinduism*, trans. Fohr & Bethell, 2004, Hillsdale NY, Sophia Perennis, 3, commenting on *Katha Upanishad* 1.3.1:

> The "cavern" is no other than the cavity of the heart, which represents the place of the union of the individual with the Universal, or of the "ego" with the "self."

[26] *K.*328, *FZ.*7:338.

ularly so when the masculine is governed by rationalist thought. Blake portrays the feminine appropriately: loving, caring, tending, spinning and, generally, passive—although this passivity is accompanied by results when all aspects of the microcosm are in their rightful place. This is the major point of the tale. Neither passivity nor activity is any use on its own. Each requires the other in order to achieve transcendence, which is the ultimate goal. The story behind *The Four Zoas* concerns the usurpation of control by Reason—Urizen—from the central and most important part of the human composite, the Spiritual Imagination, Urthona. When man is governed by reason, then all his other attributes—Love, the Senses, and the Poetic Imagination—no longer function in their correct manner.

The major point to remember concerning this separation is that it is what Blake sees as occurring within each individual, male or female, when reason usurps the place of imagination. When reason governs love, sensuality and, most importantly, the imagination within any male or female, then Urizen has won and as individuals (microcosms) and as nations (macrocosms) we no longer function as was intended. Blake rages against the rise of rationalistic thought and materialistic ideas which supplant spirituality:

> I turn my eyes to the Schools & Universities of Europe
> And there behold the Loom of Locke, whose Woof rages dire,
> Wash'd by the Water-wheels of Newton: black the cloth
> In heavy wreathes folds over every Nation: cruel Works
> Of many Wheels I view, wheel without wheel, with cogs tyrannic
> Moving by compulsion each other, not as those in Eden, which,
> Wheel within wheel, in freedom revolve in harmony & peace.[27]

The notion that man's reasoning power is, or should be, supreme, is where Blake disagrees with Milton. Blake regarded Milton,

[27] K. 636, J.15:15.

Spenser, and himself as inheritors of a symbolic poetic line opposing this. But where Milton, although agreeing with Blake on the
holiness of sex—that is, that it was one of the joys of Paradise—
placed Love in the place of Reason, Blake corrected what he saw
as Milton's error and placed Love in the Loins. In the final Night
of *The Four Zoas*, Blake demonstrates the correct place for Love:

> Luvah & Vala, henceforth you are Servants; obey & live.
> You shall forget your former state; return, & Love in peace,
> Into your place, the place of seed, not in the brain or heart.[28]

Traditions other than Christian have not lost sight of the empowerment that is a feminine characteristic. In the feminine emanation of Enitharmon, Blake creates a Shakti-figure:

> Where is Shakti? It is in all. It is the left half of Shiva. Shiva is
> consciousness; Shakti is energy. Shiva is the tongue; Shakti
> is the power of speech. Shiva and Shakti live together, but
> Shiva cannot materialize himself into actions and things
> without the active cooperation of Shakti. Therefore, Shakti
> is the subject matter of tantra shastra, whether Shakti tantra
> or Shaiva tantra. Although Shakti is depicted in a feminine
> frame, hailed as a goddess, described as a beautiful lady, the
> tantras unanimously declare that Shakti is the all-pervading
> and all-embracing existence in a saint and a sinner, in a man
> and a woman, in a believer and in a non-believer.[29]

It is through Enitharmon's heart's gates that Los is able to start
mankind on its journey towards union. By combining, they are
able to form a world where they can produce mankind, their offspring:

> ...Los unwearied labour'd
> The immortal lines upon the heavens, till with sighs of love,
> Sweet Enitharmon mild, Entranc'd breath'd forth upon the
> wind
> The spectrous dead. Weeping, the Spectres view'd the
> immortal Works

[28] K.366, FZ. 9:363.
[29] Swami Sivananda Saraswati and Swami Satyananda Saraswati, *Devi:
Honouring Shakti*, 2003, Munger, Bihar: Sivananda Math, 39.

Of Los, Assimilating to those forms, Embodied & Lovely
In youth & beauty, in the arms of Enitharmon mild repos-
ing.[30]

Blake is never just speaking of the physical act, the sexual climax.
By placing love in the loins of the microcosm, humanity, Blake is
not reducing love to mere sexual pleasure. We must read this as
union with God in the same manner as the mystics speak of their
union with God.[31] Just as the embrace of the Loathly Bride by
the King, or King to be, empowers him and provides through her
dominion the ability to rule, so Enitharmon is the active power
who enables Los to commence reconstruction of the world, saving those souls within it from the barrenness of a world governed
by reason.[32]

I argue that Blake understood, intuitively and intellectually,
that this was what was hidden in Christian religion and that he
attempted to rectify what he saw as a loss by rewriting Genesis to
Revelation in his poem *The Four Zoas*. The method he chose for
this poem was to make England, the country, a macrocosm for
the individual inhabitants of that country. Albion, England, the
macrocosm, is not complete or functioning in the correct spiritual manner without his feminine emanation, Jerusalem. Just so,
the microcosms that are the Four Zoas of the poem—each and
every individual male and female who make up the population of
Albion—are also unable to function spiritually without union of
the male and female aspects. Each Zoa is named and appointed a

---

[30] *K.*332, *FZ.*7:470.

[31] As Evelyn Underhill observes, "It was natural and inevitable that the
imagery of human love and marriage should have seemed to the mystic the
best of all images of his own "fulfilment of life," his soul's surrender, first to
the call, finally to the embrace of Perfect Love" *Mysticism*, 1990, New York,
Bantam Doubleday Dell (136). The Jewish belief that the physical union in
marriage is a *mitzvah* has been noted above; and the mystical conception of
the Spiritual Marriage is also important in Islam (thus Underhill, op. cit., 92).

[32] Ananda Coomaraswamy, *Traditional Art and Symbolism*, ed. Roger Lipsey,
1989, Princeton, Princeton University Press, 357. In Coomaraswamy's words,
she is "Dominion; not the Ruler himself, but the Power, the Glory and the Fortune with which he operates."

particular aspect of the human: Urizen/Reason, Tharmas/Body, Luvah/Love/Hate and Urthona, Spiritual Imagination.

> Four Mighty ones are in every Man; a Perfect Unity
> Cannot Exist but from the Universal Brotherhood of Eden,
> The Universal Man, to Whom be Glory Evermore. Amen.[33]

Urthona has no tangible presence in the material world. Instead he, as the deepest part of the microcosm, the Spirit, is represented in the material world by Los, "the Vehicular Form of strong Urthona,"[34] whose aspect is Poetic Imagination. The importance of Urthona to Blake is shown by his division in the material world. As the Spirit, he does not enter this world but is represented by the personas of Los and Enitharmon, the only Zoa so represented. From the start of the poem this division is shown. In Eden, Los is known as Urthona; in the world of generation, he is known as Los.[35] Urizen, Luvah, and Tharmas—and their respective emanations, Ahania, Vala, and Enion—are present in the world of generation. But it is only Urthona who divides into Spectre, Shadow, Emanation, and the active principle in this world, Los. When Los, the Poetic Imagination, acknowledges Urizen as "King of the Heavenly hosts" in Night the Fourth,[36] and then seeks to take Urizen's place, he effectively divides Poetic Imagination from Urthona, the Spiritual Imagination. What is left is but a shadow of what was. For Blake, the separation of poetry from its divine inspiration was the worst that could happen to mankind.

> A Poet, a Painter a Musician, an Architect: the Man Or Woman who is not one of these is not a Christian.[37]

These four Zoas make up the masculine traits as identified by Blake's mythology. But each Emanation of the individual Zoa has attributes and traits that make up the feminine aspect. Ahania/

---

[33] K. 264, FZ. 1:9.

[34] K. 684; J. 53:1.

[35] "Los was the fourth immortal starry one, & in the Earth/ Of a bright Universe, Empery attended day & night, Days & nights of revolving joy. Urthona was his name / In Eden" (K. 264, FZ.1:14).

[36] K. 298, FZ. 4:38.

[37] K. 776.

Urizen is Pleasure, Enion/Tharmas is Generative Instinct, Vala/
Luvah is Emotions, and Enitharmon/Los is Spiritual Beauty.[38]
These first three feminine aspects are lost to the poem by Night
the Seventh, and remain only as distant voices. These are the four
aspects of the human being and the four aspects of the cosmos.
The importance of this fourfold division of the microcosm, man,
which is repeated with the division into the feminine aspects,
cannot be ignored in Blake's mythology. It is the foundation for
his spiritual beliefs and his poetry.

Los and Enitharmon represent the Spirit and Soul of all mankind and each individual. Their warring and divisions, which are
often indicative of male/female relationships, and subsequent
reunion, are symbolic of what individual humans must seek. The
soul, the mutable, mortal part of the human composite, achieves
salvation only upon surrender to the constant immortal part,
which is the spirit-intellect. The most obvious choice for representation of this union in the mortal world is the union of male
and female, but this does not signify submission by the female,
for, as the Upanishad says, "This self gives itself to that self, and
that self to this self." Each human contains these two parts and
surrenders the part that is mutable in order to achieve salvation.
In *The Four Zoas* this union is demonstrated by Los and Enitharmon when Enitharmon bears the Spectre of Urthona into
the heart of Los. The embrace which then takes place allows the
reunion of the four plus four parts of the microcosm.

> I already feel a World within,
> Opening its gates, & in it all the real substances
> Of which these in the outward World are shadows which
> pass away.[39]

Blake chose the roles of female and male to represent duality.
This is the case regardless whether Blake is to be regarded as
Gnostic or not. It is a traditional manner of thought that predates

---

[38] Thus Foster Damon, op. cit., 124: "Enitharmon is Spiritual Beauty, the
twin, consort, and inspiration of the poet Los. . . . Her emblem is the Moon;
her outstanding emotion is Pity."

[39] K. 329, FZ. 7:364.

Christian theology.[40] Blake uses Enitharmon's heart's gates; Parmenides uses the gates of the paths of night and day through which the "man of knowledge" must pass; Odysseus is told of the Clashing Rocks (Symplegades) in Homeric myth: the examples are as many as the mythologies. It is through the Gates of Enitharmon's heart that Los must pass before any acceptance of opposites is able to take place; but the gates of Enitharmon's heart are contained within each and every individual.

> And thine the Human Face & thine
> The Human Hands & Feet & Breath
> Entering thro' the Gates of Birth
> And passing thro' the Gates of Death.[41]

The symbolism of passage through gates or doors is that of the separation of one polarity from another: the Gates of Birth lead into the mortal, generated destructible world; and it is through the Gates of Death that the immortal, indestructible spirit is found. The Gates of Death are therefore also the Gates of Birth, or Life, as the passage through these gates causes death to the flesh and birth to the spirit.

But entry through these gates can only take place if the emotion of pity, an emotion designated by Blake as belonging to the feminine, is allowed to function in the right manner. For Blake, pity is the means by which this may be achieved; but this does not mean Blake was unaware of both interpretations of the word."[42] When the Gates of Enitharmon's heart are opened by the emotion of pity—the feminine attribute—the union of the opposing

---

[40] See Denis Saurat, *Blake & Modern Thought*, 1964, New York, Russell & Russell, 4, who argues that the lower classes were always at odds with the ruling orders of the Church; this, he says, leads to various types of heretical beliefs including Gnosticism. Blake's first biographer, Alexander Gilchrist, op. cit., also attributed Gnostic beliefs to Blake. E. P. Thompson's last book, *Witness Against the Beast: William Blake and the Moral Law*, 1993, Cambridge, Cambridge University Press, raises the question of Blake's adherence to the Muggletonians. I remain committed to the idea that Blake's beliefs were *sui generis*.

[41] K. 651, J.27:57.

[42] Refer to discussion on page 11 re: Pity.

members of microcosm and macrocosm is able to take place. As Meister Eckhart states: "I stand at the door and wait . . . thou needst not seek Him here or there: He is no farther off than the door of the heart."[43]

That Blake chooses the feminine as the place for this virtue elevates the role of the female far above any apparent reduction of status in the material world. The emotion of pity, a female characteristic, when felt in its true sense, allows the recognition of the divine within each person to take place; but equally importantly, allows the recognition of the divine by another person to occur. But, of course, this role is only of importance if the reader values the idea of spiritual worth, not where "Soul and all teachings about soul (that soul began as immortal or else expects to attain immortality)" are considered "not simply laughable but even illusory."[44] Blake's resolution in *The Four Zoas* is through the feminine, which is contained within everyone, and which he personifies as Enitharmon,

> For Man cannot unite with Man but by their Emanations,
> Which stand both Male & Female at the Gates of each
> Humanity.[45]

Enitharmon is a most traditional hero. It is through her and of her that life and life-thereafter come into being. Through pity, she breathes life into mortals and is the maker of manifestation.[46] Through pity, the union between male and female is able to take place, a union that allows for an acceptance of contrary states of being. Male and female—Los and Enitharmon—represent contrary states of being in this world; and for Blake, acceptance of contrary states of being is the essential first step towards recognition of the divine present within all. Non-acceptance of these

---

[43] Underhill, op. cit., 133.

[44] *Asclepius*, 24, n.1.

[45] K.733, J. 88:10.

[46] Blake again used traditional symbology in the creation of this role for Enitharmon, echoing what is to be found in the *Tantra-tattva*, where the male and female, light and dark, earth and sky dualities are designated Shiva and Shakti; see e.g., M. Eliade, *Myths, Dreams and Mysteries*, 1975, New York, Harper & Row, 144.

states is the Negation that must be destroyed. The union of opposites which takes place has, of course, a signification that has not escaped the attention of traditionalists, although our contemporary society has trouble accepting this position. Alan Watts has observed that "a sexually self-conscious culture such as our own must beware of its natural tendency to see religion as a symbolizing of sex, for to sexually uncomplicated people it has always been obvious that sex is the symbol of religion."[47]

The sense of touch is of such importance to Blake that it is not allocated to one particular aspect of the human being, or Zoa. Without the emotion of pity, in the sense expressed in "The Divine Image," touching cannot take place. Or to put this more clearly, touching is only able to take place on a purely physical level. Without pity, touching only allows the recognition of just this self, the selfhood, thus becoming a purely singular and selfish activity. When acknowledgement of the divine in the other and the self takes place, the embrace transports both selves past the warring state to that of acceptance and union. This is why Watts says "sex is the symbol of religion" to those who are not constrained by self-consciousness. This selfhood, this "incrustation," can only be removed by the practise of Divine Pity or Piety, which is the feminine attribute that all possess but that is designated as Enitharmon's attribute. In the creation of Enitharmon, Blake has presented us with a traditional female figure that directly ties back into the Earth Mother. Enitharmon is a paradigmatic figure linked to both birth and death. Millennia after *The Hymn to Demeter* was written, the search by the spirit for union with the soul is recreated by Blake in the actions of the Four Zoas and their Emanations. To paraphrase Schuon, esoterism is the principle under which Blake wrote. We, as readers, have an obligation to find the way as we study these more ancient works.

---

[47] Alan Watts, *Myth and Ritual in Christianity,* 1968, Boston, Beacon Press, 17.

PART TWO

Woman as Goddess
in Pre-History

3

The Goddess,
Woman, and Birth

IN OUR PRE-HISTORY, before anything was written down, life on earth was celebrated by recognition of the female and, in particular, of the feminine ability to bring forth another life. She was known by many different names and is still present in many cultures and religions. The archaic time has been investigated by many and from many various backgrounds and points of view. Archaeologists have excavated the dwellings, and scholars have studied the myths; and after them come the interpreters; religious, Jungian, Feminist, Marxist, and so on. This will be just one more interpretation. The questions of who this "Mother Goddess" was and why she provokes these responses will remain.

Günther Zuntz says, "this is the oldest godhead perceived by mankind,"[1] where the feminine attribute of physical creation was revered and an object of wonder. This celebration is less evident today. More often in modern western society the act of re-creation is mundane and governed by scientific means. Zuntz places the deification of woman much earlier than others, who link it with the onset of agriculture. Irrespective of when this occurs it merits our attention. His work deals primarily with the megalithic ruins in Malta and Gozo, islands where faith is maintained today through the worship in numerous churches.[2] Here, the schisms and doubts that beset the industrialized, rationalized world outside did not penetrate and subjugate their belief. Here,

---

[1] Günther Zuntz, *Persephone. Three Essays on Religion and Thought in Magna Graecia*, 1971, Oxford, Clarendon Press, 13.

[2] Zuntz, ibid., 4.

on this *isola sacra*,[3] Ishtar, Isis, Persephone/Demeter, or any of the countless unnamed and unknown goddesses, moved easily through Eve into Mary. Blake's couplet accurately describes the movement of life through the female.

> There is a Void outside of Existence, which if enter'd into
> Englobes itself & becomes a Womb.[4]

From the void, outside of existence, comes the womb and comes the child. From the womb comes life, and this was and is to be celebrated.

Modern biological explanations have further removed wonder or speculation from birth. When Megalithic trefoil ground plan structures honoring the Great Mother were built in Malta there was no question as to what was being honored.[5] Woman, in all her fecund splendor, was revered in the very construction of the place of worship. Originally then, particularly in Malta, the divine is overwhelmingly feminine. This honoring of the female also occurred with the Lycians, for example, who were originally from Crete. As Herodotus says,

> in one of their customs, that of taking the mother's name
> instead of the father's, they are unique. Ask a Lycian who he
> is, and he will tell you his own name and his mother's, then
> his grandmother's and great-grandmother's and so on.[6]

Many attempts have been made to reconcile women's position, sometimes favorably, sometimes less so, to that of men. There was even one important attempt made by a man. Johann Jakob Bachofen, writing in 1861 and without the benefits of modern archaeology, relied upon the stories found in ancient myths to

[3] Zuntz, ibid., Zuntz quotes T. Zammit, *Prehistoric Malta* (1930), 132, ("the holy island of neolithic faith"), n.1.

[4] K.620, J.1:1.

[5] Zuntz, op. cit., 8:

The so-called "trefoil" signifies the womb of the Mother (its rear-bay—no doubt the cultic *sanctum sanctorum*—intimating the rest of her body, perhaps the head), and that in the final type the womb is represented by the larger, first hall: the nurturing breasts, by the second.

[6] Herodotus, *The Histories*, trans. de Sélincourt, 1984, Middlesex, Penguin Books, 1:174.

build his theories.[7] We might say, perhaps, that he was an opti-
mist, but it is not his optimism that brings him into disfavor with
contemporary writers. What Bachofen said had religious conno-
tations. His findings, extrapolated from myth, placed women in
the position of rulers of a matriarchal society in pre-Homeric society. This may seem to be a view that modern women might welcome, but his faith in religion appears to be a major sticking point
for contemporary readers; and he had a theory of progress, of various stages we must pass through until we finally get it right—
which is also a problem. Bachofen's "getting it right" is seen by
today's society as paternalism.[8] Doherty regards Bachofen's position on women as anathema and dislikes what she names as his
"pedestalian" stance regarding the female sex. But men must also
strive to achieve their position on the pedestal. This does not happen by virtue of being born male. As with Bachofen, Doherty is a
product of her time.

The idea that matriarchal rule was "right" is wrong, as indeed
is the idea of patriarchal rule. Both sexes, female and male, the
soul and the spirit within each individual human being, must be
functioning together for the human being, female or male, and
the society itself, to function in its correct manner. This is the
ideal, and it is apparently an ideal impossible to achieve. **While
we may point to a utopian expectation on the part of Bachofen
concerning the abilities of his society, or indeed ours, with no
ideal society itself is the poorer.** It is likely that Bachofen saw the
roles of female and male as symbiotic in the same manner as
Blake. Without the spirit, the soul is only a material thing that

---

[7] Rosemary Radford Ruether, *Goddesses and the Divine Feminine*, 2006, CA,
University of California Press, 254–255. This following quote, which supplies us
with some background regarding Bachofen, is taken from *Goddesses and the
Divine Feminine*:

Johann Jakob Bachofen (1815–1887). A Swiss Jurist and historian of Roman law,
Bachofen was fascinated by ancient Greek and Roman mythology, which he
believed accurately reflected the social evolution of ancient society, from the pre-
Greek cultures of the Mediterranean to Greek classical society, culminating in the
Roman empire.

[8] Lillian E. Doherty, *Gender and the Interpretation of Classical Myth*, 2001,
London, Gerald Duckworth, 115.

dies. For Blake, as well as Bachofen, "transcendent spirituality" was the sole aim for the human being of both male and female gender.

The greater mystery associated with the female is the primary mystery of death, and this appears to have been associated with her from early times. If the feminine is associated with the production of the physical, then it follows, by the logic of contrariety, that she must be associated with its destruction. This is not quite to throw over the principles of non-contradiction, but to recognize that quite contrary propositions are more closely related to each other than almost any others. The feminine is most firmly aligned with the material world, and therefore with decay.[9] This is allied with the ability to create life from oneself, and nurture that life; and it goes hand in hand with death. When woman gives birth to a child, no matter if she is surrounded by countless people dancing attendance or alone in a field, she faces by herself the lesser mystery of life. The carrying of the child, and ultimately the birth itself, belong only to the mother. Finally we all face the Greater Mystery, that is, Death—but all women who give birth to children in a normal manner face that lesser mystery at the moment of birth. There is no one between you, the mother, and that moment. This does give women a differing perception of life to that of men, and may well have led to man's recognition of the greater knowledge belonging to women in prehistory. Such an acknowledgment of their importance is present in the Oglala Lakota tradition. Joseph Epes Brown tells us that, for the Oglala Lakota, when a young girl menstruates for the first time, rites are performed to instruct her regarding her power.[10] Thus, upon becoming a woman, the young girl is made to realize her important links with Mother Earth. Her power is so strong that from the time of and at her menses she could damage the power of the holy man who has worked continuously to achieve his power by means of meditation. By contrast the female power

---

[9] Although we must not forget Macbeth here, where the feminine principle—the witches, Lady Macbeth, sleep—acts against the baby innocent.

[10] Joseph Epes Brown, *The Sacred Pipe*, 1989, Norman, University of Oklahoma Press, 116.

is arrived at by purely physiological means but this does not mean that it is to be used lightly.

So important and unavoidable are these physiological stages in the life of a woman—menses, fecundity, birth, post-menses, death—that men may have marked the stages in their own development to mirror them. The initiation rites in traditional societies were undertaken by all men, starting at puberty; and they were formalized, that is, instruction was given on how to accommodate the power and rights of being male. This process of initiation is also true for all major religions. But more often than not, modern males and females in developed countries introduce themselves to being adult without instruction from their elders. Both sexes necessarily undergo change at puberty, but for a woman there are no alternatives to the ongoing changes that occur. Even if she turns her back on the material world and retires to a cloister, the physical changes continue to remind her of her role. The post-menses time should see a woman withdraw from the physicality of her fecund stage and develop a more contemplative mode of behavior, which is not necessarily an option for the male. Her physical development is a part of life, and while society and science have done their best to alter and control these changes, nevertheless they still occur. This has led to an effort to undermine, devalue, control, and replace these changes.

Marija Gimbutas (1921–1994) was born in Vilnius, Lithuania. Her approach to archaeology differed from the (predominantly) masculine offerings because she thought it was the archaeologist's role to interpret the data. In any scientific discipline this is frowned upon as being without rigor. That any human being, male or female, is able to divorce their self from their study is unlikely, if not undesirable. Claiming that the discipline requires this seems folly. As Blake says in *The Mental Traveller*, "the Eye altering alters all."[11] From an archaeological viewpoint there are many intimations that the Great Mother was important through the periods 7000–3000 BC. In support of this, Gimbutas finds that the countless statues of females—predominantly pregnant—of what could be deities, woman and bird symbols dated 7th and 6th

[11] *K.* 426, *MT*: 62.

49

millennia, moon goddesses, snake goddesses, and the cosmic or primordial egg, all support this proposition. For Gimbutas there is a distinction between the Indo-Europeans, who saw the Goddess as an Earth mother, and the Old Europeans, who saw her as a snake and Bird Goddess, as water and air divinities.[12] Gimbutas offers archaeological evidence to support her theories. To question her on this level is beyond my competence. Nevertheless I am unsurprised by the reactions of her colleagues and those who want a definitive answer to the vexed question concerning the role of women. Her colleagues have chosen to criticize her for her spiritual awareness; the feminists for her lack of militancy. As Doherty says.

> At stake are these women's credentials as archaeologists, their chances of publication and their very jobs. It seems especially important to them to repudiate the conclusions of Gimbutas, the only well-known and (formerly) respected archaeologist to have embraced the Goddess spirituality movement. In the Goddess literature, Gimbutas is universally cited as an authority; in the archaeological literature, article after article, book after book bring her forward as the example to be avoided: the scholar who became a "true believer"—and thereby ceased to be a scholar.[13]

[12] Marija Gimbutas, *The Gods and Goddesses of Old Europe—7000 to 3500 BC, Myths, Legends and Cult Images*, 1974, London, Thames and Hudson, 152:

"Fertility Goddess" or "Mother Goddess" is a more complex image than most people think. She was not only the Mother Goddess who commands fertility, or the Lady of the Beasts who governs the fecundity of animals and all wild nature, or the frightening Mother Terrible, but a composite image with traits accumulated from both the pre-agricultural and agricultural eras. During the latter she became essentially a Goddess of Regeneration, i.e., a Moon Goddess, product of a sedentary, matrilinear community, encompassing the archetypal unity and multiplicity of feminine nature. She was the giver of life and all that promotes fertility, and at the same time she was the wielder of the destructive powers of nature. The feminine nature, like the moon, is light as well as dark.

[13] Radford Ruether, *Goddesses and the Divine Feminine*, op. cit.,7:

On the other hand, new conflicts between various feminist perspectives have also arisen. In the 1980s, Goddess feminists appropriated the work of archaeologist Marija Gimbutas as proof of prehistoric matriarchal or matricentric societies overthrown by invading patriarchalists, a viewpoint popularly disseminated by writers

The rise of matriarchy or Mother Right occurs for Bachofen when agrarian societies are founded. Bachofen is confident that this makes the rule of these societies matriarchal, thus causing the reaction that occurred in Greek and Roman societies.[14] While there may have been greater emphasis placed upon the role of women then, Mircea Eliade sees that the roots of this go further back, while acknowledging that the perception of women deepens:

> To be sure, feminine and maternal sacrality was not unknown in the Paleolithic, but the discovery of agriculture markedly increases its power. The sacrality of sexual life, and first of all of feminine sexuality, becomes inseparable from the miraculous enigma of creation. Parthenogenesis, the *hieros gamos*, and ritual orgy express, on different planes, the religious character of sexuality.[15]

The role of women as tillers of the field, and therefore those responsible for the fertility of the crops, elevates their position in society. As fecund females responsible for the food of the community, they return to the maternal home after marriage as described by Eliade, but this is matrilocation rather than matriarchy as proposed by Bachofen and Zuntz. It cannot however be fully known whether societies in which the Mother Goddess was honored were matriarchal, matrilocal, matrilineal—but given the reaction of Greek and Roman societies, Bachofen may be correct. What arises from the rule of Mother Right is "Demetrian morality," a sharp contrast to "Aphroditean hetaerism," which belongs

such as Charlene Spretnak and Riane Eisler. The emerging community of feminist paleo-archaeologist, alarmed by what they saw as bad archaeology, responded with a critique of Gimbutas's work. They sought to define a feminist archaeological standpoint that was neither an argument for recovery of original matriarchy nor a defense of universal patriarchy. This academic critique, popularized by writers such as Cynthia Eller, led to renewed charges of "betrayal" from Goddess feminists.

See also Doherty, Lillian E. op. cit., 1.

[14] Johann Jakob Bachofen, *Myth, Religion, and Mother Right*, trans. Manheim, 1967, London Routledge & Kegan Paul, 75.

[15] Mircea Eliade, *A History of Religious Ideas*, trans. Trask, 3 Vols., 1978, Chicago, University of Chicago Press. i., 40–41.

to the pre-agricultural society. Demeter gave us agriculture and her mysteries where the mortal soul was represented by her daughter, Persephone. With Demetrian morality, εὐκοσμια— "good order"—is imposed upon primordial disorder.[16] For Bachofen, since the family structure was not present in the same manner for pre-agricultural societies, mothers did not necessarily love their children in the same way. Perhaps they loved all children of the group to which they belonged. But the Demetrian mother-love extended recognition to their daughters and through them recognition of the maternal line took place. This is the basis of Bachofen's argument: there was a necessity for daughters to be endowered by their families, as opposed to going out to earn their dowries by being paid for sexual services, which is hetaerism.[17] As a reaction to such usage, Bachofen argues that the next development is the rise of Amazonism, which he links with hetaerism.[18] Amazonism is an extreme example of matriarchy. Bachofen states that Amazonism necessarily followed hetaerism because the degradation suffered by women in a hetaeric society must be addressed.[19] Again circumstances changed: the mother was recognized to an extent, enabling women—and therefore society—to live a more moral life. Thus Demetrian law was of benefit to the entire society and these changes in circumstances occurred when society itself was settled. When hunters and gatherers were replaced by farmers, even the natural symbols associated with them altered.

Bachofen is right in allocating the natural world to the female. That he attributes this only to the time of Mother Right does not mean that these characteristics disappear. Acknowledgment of these characteristics is present in all cultures, for "under the moon the law of matter prevails, with death assigned as twin brother to

[16] Bachofen, op. cit., 97.

[17] Herodotus, op. cit., 80:

Working-class girls in Lydia prostitute themselves without exception to collect money for their dowries, and continue the practice until they marry. They choose their own husband. . . . Apart from the fact that they prostitute their daughters, the Lydian way of life is not unlike our own.

[18] Bachofen, op. cit.,104.

[19] Ibid.,105.

all life."[20] As Blake's void "outside of existence" becomes a womb, so for the Oglala Lakota:

> Seeds sprout in the darkness of the ground before they know the summer and the day. In the night of the womb the spirit quickens into flesh.[21]

Or, in Kabir's words:

> The distinction of the Conditioned from the Unconditioned is but a word:
> The Unconditioned is the seed, the Conditioned is the flower and the fruit.
> Knowledge is the branch, and the Name is the root.
> Look, and see where the root is: happiness shall be yours when you come to the root.
> The root will lead you to the branch, the leaf, the flower, and the fruit: (LXXX) [22]

In Classical Greece, Bachofen accurately describes the replacement of Demeter by Dionysus. When Dionysus usurps the position of Demeter, his role is that of a hetaeric god replacing a matriarchal one. Bachofen's point is that as mankind seeks to improve its behavior, this is reflected in the godhead—although it is difficult to see an improvement in the followers of Dionysus.[23] The women in the train of Dionysus were more likely those who had supported Demeter, whose wrested victory from the sky gods—when she held the world in her hand and prevented human recognition of the Olympian gods—thus becomes a hollow one. Although seeming to support Demeter, Dionysus is undermining the most important tenets of her religion. He is a sky god, not chthonic as she is, but he claims her position.[24] Bachofen's argument is that the rise of Dionysus occurs in response to perceived Amazonism, that is, that Demetrian motherhood and marriage has become too powerful in masculine eyes. As a consequence of

[20] Bachofen, op. cit., 127.
[21] Neihardt, op. cit., 177.
[22] Kabir, op. cit., 86.
[23] Bachofen, op. cit., 98.
[24] Ibid., 100.

this reaction, Demeter, and both male and female, are debased, their positions reduced to that of being pleasure-seekers with the enjoyment of sexual pleasure as their creed, although still within the confines of marriage. Northrop Frye says: "Mastery over woman produces the same morbidity and imaginative idleness as mastery over man." One may be master and the other servant, but both are debased by this relationship. This is a return to the hetaeric state for women, and thus a downgrading of their position. Demeter's links with Dionysus are replaced by his stronger links with Aphrodite, developing a "sensualization of existence." Bachofen links Dionysus with democracy, the "undifferentiated mass," which brings with it the reduction of belief, thought, and practice to the lowest common factor.

There is a further link with the new democracy in Aeschylus's trilogy, the *Oresteia*. In the third play, the *Eumenides*, when Aeschylus allows Apollo to state that the mother is not the true parent of the child—that her role is merely to take care of the seed for the father who is the true parent—he sets one pattern for what follows. Matricide will go unpunished because Apollo's analogy with the "empty vessel," an analogy that must have been at odds with the better judgement of at least fifty percent of the population, was so successful that Athene's court of judgement was installed, the Erinyes become the Eumenides, and everyone lived happily ever after. Apollo, as "lord of the great temple-cave," is honored by the Chorus for supporting Orestes in this matter of matricide. Apollo, particularly because of his Delphic role, represents feminine, chthonic justice as well as masculine, heavenly justice; and his judgement here does not reflect this balance. But Aeschylus was not writing in a vacuum. He was merely restating a position held by some ancient Greeks, as shown by the treatment of women in the *Iliad*. Thomas Aquinas and Aristotle are held responsible for introducing this false position into Christianity in Rosemary Radford Ruether's article, "Catholicism, Woman, Body and Sexuality: A Response."[25] But this was first formulated

[25] Rosemary Radford Ruether, *Women, Religion and Sexuality*, ed. Jeanne Becher, "Catholicism, Woman, Body and Sexuality: A Response" 1991, Philadelphia, Trinity Press International, 222:

by Aeschylus, some one hundred years before Aristotle, who made the same error regarding woman as only a receptacle for the seed. What this illustrates is the widespread nature of that belief in Greek society and, as Radford Ruether has shown, upon our contemporary society through the teachings of the Church. If every birth is divine, an act of the goddess, as it was in pre-history, this is also acknowledged in Christianity. But this divine act became merely service to patriarchy through the mind-set shown in the *Iliad*, the plays of Aeschylus, and the writings of Aristotle.

Why is acceptance of two sexes as advocated by Blake not paramount in our contemporary Western society? Erich Neumann's theory traces the Great Mother, the archetype, through developing societies. For him, the World Mother remains in contemporary society because she is an archetype even though the symbol is overlaid by patriarchal meanings. For Neumann, who is a Jungian, the answer is the lack of "psychic wholeness," whereas the more appropriate term would be "spiritual wholeness." But even this critic of Western males is reticent about using such a term. [26] But there is at least some recognition of the "divine" within his work. What has occurred in contemporary society is recognition of the female in a particular way. This has been achieved primarily through militant action on the part of women. But that recognition brings a greater loss, a loss reflected throughout society and through the division felt between the sexes.

This denial of women's equal human status with men is extended in the teachings of Thomas Aquinas, who remains the normative theologian for the Roman Catholic tradition. Thomas took over a (false) biological theory from Aristotle that taught that the male alone contributed formative potency in reproduction. The female is only the passive incubator of the male seed which is identified with the embryo. Aristotle believed that every male seed would normally produce a male. Females are born only through a defect in gestation in which the male seed fails to fully form the female matter. The result is a defective human being or woman. Women are physically weaker, less capable of moral will power or intellectual acumen than males. Their defective nature, morally, mentally and physically, makes them non-normative humans, unable to represent the fullness of human nature. They cannot exercise dominion in society, but must be governed by the male as their head. This is not how Plato saw the role of women.

[26] Erich Neumann, *The Great Mother An Analysis of the Archetype*, 1963, Princeton, Princeton University Press, xlii.

The Homeric representation of the feminine as seen in the *Iliad* and the *Odyssey* provides contrasting views. In the *Iliad*, the strengths of the female are represented by the goddesses, whereas the mortal women sung are representative of weakness. In contrast, in the *Odyssey*, Odysseus is dependent upon female help—both godly and mortal—to achieve his physical goal of returning to Ithaca. The nurturing mother figure is represented by Circe, Calypso, Queen Arete, Penelope, Eurycleia, Anticleia, his mother, and Athene. The *Iliad* is thus representative of masculine dominance, while the *Odyssey* is the opposite. The method of presenting opposites to achieve a resolution is often employed by the Greeks. I would argue that this characteristic means of proposing opposition actually underlies these two epics. Blake said, "Without Contraries is no progression." Odysseus is not just striving to achieve his physical goal of reaching home, but is also a man searching for spiritual growth. He achieves this rebirth in Book XIII, under the auspices of the feminine, in this case the eternal virgin.

Although one might question the aims for a "higher life" of the women who sought the right to vote, or the right to equal pay and recognition of their position in society, the methods chosen by them to achieve these aims—while not "armed resistance"—were often regarded by their male counterparts as Amazonian, or more probably in today's society, as lesbian. On Bachofen's plan for the development of a society, these women were resisting a hetaeric use of themselves and the next step would be a Demetrian society. Of course this will not necessarily follow. Those social changes were wrought by a humanity looking for an ideal that had a religious basis other than the hetaeric ideal and of sacred prostitution. One thing we may say about today's society is that, whether ruled by male or female, it will not have a religious basis.

But perhaps the basic argument remains true. When women are subjugated, used as tools for men's pleasure, denied the right to be regarded as more than receptacles, what may follow is an upsurge of militant feeling. We can look back through history and witness these patterns of behavior. The Emancipationists were certainly looked upon as militant by their society. They did not take up and bear arms in the manner of the Amazons, but they did resist the laws of the land. For Wollstonecraft, who wrote *A Vindication of the Rights of Women,* women were nothing more than chattels, with no right to own property, to divorce from an unhappy or violent marriage, or to vote for a Member of Parliament who would support her claims; and their most common means of financial support was through prostitution, either within or without marriage. There is no doubt that Wollstonecraft was responding to very real problems within her society, but her response was just that. The solution to these problems could be attained by changing the physical conditions experienced by women. William Blake wrote *Visions of the Daughters of Albion* in response to these material problems, which included slavery. He saw that the changing of physical conditions would never be enough. Of the three protagonists in his poem, those who never escape the bondage of the physical world they occupy are male, while the female is given the ability to recognize the "centre of sweet delight" within herself and thus is able to escape spiritually.

In the *Oresteia,* Aeschylus could well have been putting into words a reaction that was present within his own society. Women were too much in control and had to be made to recognize Father Right. Perhaps, if we can believe Bachofen, our present society is about to enter a new age of matriarchal rule.[27] This would mean, of course, that these systems of government not only evolve but devolve. Patriarchy provoked, by its treatment of women, a response reflected in the suffragette and women's liberation movement. If society then chooses to describe and denigrate the women's struggles as a form of Amazonism, lesbianism, or lacking in propriety, this is more indicative of the society's shortcomings than those of the women. The discovery by science of foolproof birth control has allowed a type of hetaerism to develop. From this hetaerism then, will a form of matriarchal rule follow? Surely Blake's "when Thou & I walked about, Imbodied" is a better option, an option that recognizes and accepts the need for the other.

[27] Bachofen, op. cit., 92.

When looked at from this perspective, the idea that woman was once the main source of spiritual impetus for her society becomes of little importance. And therein lies the major problem for contemporary critics. What has happened to Neumann's archetype? For Bachofen, this was the degradation of matriarchy: "The older matriarchy was a source of lofty virtues and of an existence which, though limited in its ideas, was nevertheless secure and well ordered."[28] These "lofty virtues" have been lost by the time Aeschylus was writing *The Oresteia*, and Neumann's Great Mother, the Archetype, is a distant memory.

While the worship of the Goddess—whether Great Mother or Nature—is an acceptance of the mystery that surrounds the female, it does not necessarily have a salvific connotation. Goddess worship is an acknowledgment of fecundity, of increase, of mystery, but does not promise life after death in any specific manner. What is applauded is life on earth, and the re-creation of life was quite properly idealized in the form of the feminine, and more particularly in the form of the mother.[29] This honoring of the mother, as Zuntz says, was a widely held belief shared by many differing peoples. Widespread honoring of the feminine, with particular emphasis on the ability to recreate, was a very important basis for the society of our predecessors, whether they came from Crete, Lycia, Egypt, or anywhere there was settlement. Did the males, being ignorant savages, know that they participated in any way in this miracle? Gimbutas states that there "is no evidence that in Neolithic times mankind understood biological conception,"[30] although she retracts this in her later work.[31] I

[28] Bachofen, op. cit., 103.

[29] Zuntz, op. cit., 22:

Meantime, the fact appears to be established, and is confirmed by the uninterrupted series, from many and widely distant places of the fixed symbols representing "The Mother," that her religion existed and persisted throughout the Near East, beginning at an age in relation to which the Sumerian is, to us, almost a recent past, and continuing down into the Graeco-Roman period.

[30] Gimbutas, op. cit., 237.

[31] Radford Ruether, *Goddesses and the Divine Feminine*, op. cit., 26:

I believe that whatever age Gimbutas allocates man's knowledge of participation in the birth process does not greatly matter. There is a period of some years

rather think that Neolithic man, whether Indo or Old European, had some suspicion that the penis was of importance in this act of growth. After all, wasn't he able to see with his own eyes that his member also had the attribute of growth? It might be a little naïve to imagine that the male was so bemused by the ability of the female to reproduce that he didn't extend some of that wonder to his own ability. Ananda Coomaraswamy states that anthropology tends to look at the significance of rites "in isolation."[32] He quotes an article concerning "the belief of some Pacific and Australian peoples in spiritual paternity," and then proves that the commentary demonstrates the singularity of the anthropologist rather than the "primitive" culture.[33] Coomaraswamy then shows how this belief in spiritual paternity is shared by Greek, Christian, Hindu, and Muslim. Of course, he is speaking of anthropology and not archaeology, but the same single vision is also true for archaeology. Where does this place Bachofen's belief that motherhood equals matriarchy? Can we just dismiss the idea that fecundity is the sole basis for the countless statues honoring the mother? Some are beautiful, some terrible, but all appear to honor the mother. I would think that matriarchal rule, even of a Demetrian type, was an unlikely event. Certainly, the mysteries of birth and death remain as central points to male and female at any time. But, maybe, the fecund female was just looked after, protected, fought for, because she was of the same value as a prize breeding cow is to a modern farmer. Neumann says that the

between the publishing of the two books and, maybe, a process of evolution in thought for the author. But, this is one of the sticks used to beat Gimbutas.

[32] Ananda K. Coomaraswamy, *The Bugbear of Literacy*, 1979, Middlesex, Perennial Books, 92:

Neglecting the possibility or probability that these peculiarities may not be of local origin, but may represent only provincial or peripheral survivals of theories held by some or all of the more sophisticated communities from which the primitive peoples may have declined.

[33] Coomaraswamy, ibid., 93:

The Pacific doctrine of spiritual conception is anything but an isolated phenomenon. For example, it is explicitly stated in the Buddhist canonical literature that three things are necessary for conception: the union of father and mother, the mother's period, *and the presence of the Gandharva*—the divine and solar Eros.

feminine archetype was first revered thousands of years before man was consciously able to distinguish the Great Mother and that this occurred before Hesiod's *Theogony*, the Homeric Hymns, the *Iliad* or *Odyssey*.[34] This is based upon archaeological evidence. The importance of the Great Mother and her megalithic structures is shown in Zuntz's work.[35] Bachofen says that the rise of mother worship occurs when settlement and agriculture are the norm, as at the tail end of the neolithic. But recognition of the feminine predates the megalithic time, as has been shown by Gimbutas. As Eliade says, the Ice Age "Venuses" demonstrate that the feminine was of sufficient importance that these statues were made. That we do not know, definitively, for what purpose these statues were made does not detract from their significance.[36]

For modern society, with all the benefits of scientific information, the mystery surrounding the feminine is apparently explained. Science is able to give us the physical answer to the process of creation, to the illnesses peculiar to the feminine, or the best method to rear a child. It is now even able to show any mother who is incapable of realizing this, that mitochondrial DNA is transmitted through the female line—a scientific fact that makes the position of the Lycians seem very prescient. Being female is no longer a source of wonder, let alone sacrality. And yet, still the feminine remains that unexplained other which the male seems unable to understand in any other manner but through the rational tools of science.

[34] Neumann, op. cit., 11:

The term Great Mother, as a partial aspect of the Archetypal Feminine, is a late abstraction, presupposing a highly developed speculative consciousness. And indeed, it is only relatively late in the history of mankind that we find the Archetypal Feminine designated as Magna Mater. But it was worshiped (sic) and portrayed many thousands of years before the appearance of the term.

[35] Zuntz, op. cit., 8:

The Maltese "temples" are currently designated as megalithic structures and it is today almost commonplace to regard all megalithic monuments (all, at any rate, from Northern Europe to Spain and, again, from the Canaries to Syria and Palestine) as testifying to this very concept: the devotion to the Great Mother, the Earth, as the giver and preserver of life.

[36] Eliade, *A History of Religious Ideas*, op. cit., i., 21.

What, then, do we have? Acknowledgment of the fecund female in statuary; acknowledgment of the links with Mother Earth; acknowledgment that the knowledge of life and death is made more accessible to the female through the process of giving birth; and finally, the rise of the Mother Goddess. And it appears that always allied with the perception of fecund female is the frightening aspect of fatal female. William Blake wrote the following words and put them in the mouth of Urizen, his character representing humanity's reasoning power. Urizen is speaking to his feminine emanation, Ahania.

> He groan'd anguish'd, & called her Sin,
> Kissing her and weeping over her;
> Then hid her in darkness, in silence,
> Jealous, tho' she was invisible.[37]

Ahania's answer:

> Ah, Urizen! Love!
> Flower of morning! I weep on the verge
> Of Non-entity; how wide the Abyss
> Between Ahania and thee![38]

The abyss between male and female is as wide today as it was for Urizen and Ahania. If male and female are not interdependent, then without the Soul the Spirit is aimless, and without the Spirit the Soul vanishes into non-entity.

Blake's principal female character, Enitharmon, is that feminine principle which produces the material covering, the body, for the spirit. But what makes Blake's system work is that the two contraries must coexist before any further development can happen. Neither is more important than the other. If Bachofen is correct, the replacement of matriarchal rule by patriarchal rule is not a progression but a recipe for further disaster. Blake's notion of the coexistence of opposites and their subsequent elevation beyond union seems not only more desirable, but more natural.

---

[37] K. 250, AH. 2:34.
[38] K. 254, AH. 4:52.

4

The Goddess,
Woman, and Death

WHEN ODYSSEUS visited the Kingdom of the Dead, *Book XI,*
the first spirit he encountered was that of Elpenor, a comrade
whose body had not received the traditional burial. Odysseus
was able to see the ghost of his mother, Anticleia, but he was not
to converse with her until he had spoken with Tiresias, "the
famous Theban prophet." Then Odysseus spoke with his
mother, the gentle woman who had pined and faded away
because her son did not return. After they fail in their attempt
to embrace three times, and while they exchange parting words,
a parade of beautiful, intelligent females—all of whom were
wives or daughters of princes—was brought forward by Persephone. Many of these women had mated with gods and had
borne sons who had won the type of immortality fame brings.
The fame of the women, therefore, consisted in the possession of
sufficient beauty to sexually attract a god and their ability to conceive and bear a son or two from this union, although Gods
always engender, who would then earn fame, or immortality for
the son and, indirectly, for the mother. Now there are many ways
in which this can be read. One is to see the woman as the empty
vessel that brings to fruition the seed of the god. All that is
required of her is that she has beauty enough to attract the right
lover—preferably a godly one—and the ability to entice and conceive in much the same manner as a flower will put forward
color or perfume to attract a bee. Or, one may read this as placing women in the prime role of bringing life, whether partly
divine or purely mortal, into the world—the means of ensuring
that life on this earth continues through the power of the female.

But one must ask, "why?" Why did Homer present such a parade to Odysseus, this embattled traveler who had been helped on every hand by women in his journey home? Was it merely to retell the history, mythic or otherwise, of the Greek culture? Or to reassure Odysseus and the reader that they would be as they were in the world of the dead? That, indeed, their beauty or fame would not die? The first person he meets is male, but a male for whom the proper burial requirements have not been made. Next the seer who is able to see both male and female perspectives, then his mother, the most important female in his life next to his wife, and then the parade of females, sent by Persephone herself. There is a greater significance here.

I am reminded of the help given to the "young man, companion of deathless charioteers," in the Prologue of Parmenides. The young man is accompanied by females and is journeying towards a goddess. The locked gates through which he must pass are unlocked by "cruel Justice," another goddess. The masculine aspect, represented by the young man, is only able to arrive at his destination—as is Odysseus—accompanied and educated by women and arriving at a point represented by the feminine. The spirit-intellect is assisted upon the journey to union with knowledge of the divine only by women. Justice and Right (Themis) guide Parmenides, as Athene, Circe, and Calypso guide Odysseus.[1]

In Blake's mythology of the Four Zoas, the final achievement of union with the spiritual is only achieved by the masculine entering in through the gates of the heart of the feminine. This is not a passive feminine, and one must always remember that male and female are contained within each individual human being. Blake does not allow the feminine aspect merely to accept this, for there must be an active welcoming of union, accompanied by the emotion of pity—which by this usage becomes divine, or it does not succeed. This would also appear to be true in early Greek thought. According to Blake, by entering the void, a boundless state, one chooses life as the womb closes round. From death or non-being the soul/spirit moves into being and *vice versa.* Leaving reality, we enter life through the womb.

---

[1] Parmenides' fragments.

Regaining reality, we leave through Blake's "Gates of Death," where the lowly worm builds

> ...a pillar in the mouldering church yard
> And a palace of eternity in the jaws of the hungry grave? [2]

The soul, in Plato's *Republic*, accompanied by the Daughters of Necessity, Lachesis, Clotho, and Atropos, chooses its fate. In the great void of the heavens, accompanied by the eight harmonic sirens and listening to the song of the Goddess, Necessity, souls choose their next lives and enter into existence on earth through that most feminine of organs, the womb. In this procedure that leads to birth in the material world, the Fates, who are goddesses, hold the destinies of all souls. The destinies are taken from the knees of Lachesis by a male, the Interpreter, and the process of choosing is explained by him. The choice itself is made by the individual soul. But the repository for all material life, past, present and future, resides with the female goddesses.[3]

The greater mystery associated with the female is the primary mystery of death, and according to Zuntz appears to have been connected with the feminine since pre-history. The feminine, the soul, is most firmly aligned with the material world and therefore with decay. Demeter takes Persephone back to Olympus and makes the corn grow. Their reunion allows the material world to flourish. Gimbutas argues that at the time of agricultural development, the goddess changes and she becomes "a Goddess of Regeneration," linked with the moon. Therefore there is always a light and a dark side to the feminine.[4] This is reinforcing the link between life and death that is associated with the female and is a very traditional view of the power of woman. Woman is both "unity and multiplicity," able to create life from within, and symbolic of the union of opposites. The argument that this develops only after the establishment of agriculture is rather restrictive when we look at other claims concerning the history of the development of the goddess. Gimbutas, the female author, does

[2] K. 193, VDA. 5:41, 6:1.

[3] Plato, *The Republic*, "Myth of Er," trans. Lee, ed: Rieu, 1958, Middlesex, Penguin Books, 394–401.

[4] Gimbutas, op. cit., 152.

not make claims for matriarchy, but does so for matrilinearity. Zuntz and Bachofen, both males, countenance the proposition that matriarchy was the result of this goddess worship. Zuntz agrees with Bachofen that there are grounds for believing in matriarchy because the female deity was invested with the power to originate and preserve life. Zuntz uses Çatal Hüyük, "in the Konya plain," as an illustration of how important the Mother Goddess was. He tells us that this settlement "now dated c. 6500–5650 BC," was solely devoted to the worship of her and that every four to five houses had a shrine to the Mother Goddess.[5] Here the goddess is worshipped as parturient, and the dead—as bones after the perishable flesh has been removed—are rejoined with the living, buried under the floors of the houses. Zuntz tells us that "the males are buried under the bed of the father, women and children underneath the mother's."[6] The eternal cycle is thus continually lived, "an intimate communion," which allows the acceptance of death and the recognition of renewal. As a footnote Zuntz states that Neanderthal Man practiced this custom of burial as did pre-pottery Jericho, Natufian Eynan, North Pales-

---

[5] Radford Ruether, *Goddesses and the Divine Feminine*, op. cit., 28–30. In Radford Ruether's book mention is made of the "discovery and excavation of Çatal Hüyük by the British archaeologist James Mellaart." Radford Ruether writes in defence of Mellaart, whose investigations have been taken up and enlarged by various feminist interpreters. One of these interpretations is that the figurines found are of mother goddesses, and that the sleeping platforms, higher/lower, larger/smaller, signify the importance of the female because the female remains are found under the higher and larger platforms. Another interpretation put forward by Radford Ruether concerning the figurines is that they represent the fertility of the corn, as well they might. The fertility of the corn is associated with the female very clearly in *The Hymn to Demeter*. We are not able to say concerning these earlier figurines that this fertility is not also associated with fertility in women. As to the height and size of the female platforms, this could be associated with the larger number of women and children who would occupy them, as well as putting the defenders, the men, below in order to ward off any attack—an attack which would come through the roof, as this was the only entrance. Strategically this would make them—the women and children—more expendable rather than more important. Whatever the reason for the size and position of the sleeping arrangements, does this detract from Zuntz's theory concerning the acceptance of the dead?

[6] Zuntz, op. cit., 14.

tine, neolithic Persia, and Khirokitia in Cyprus, pointing to wide-spread custom.[7] Radford Ruether does not agree with this view of Çatal Hüyük, which was discovered by a British archaeologist, James Mellaart. She says that

> Mellaart's feminist interpreters have exaggerated his descriptions considerably, claiming to see in the unbroken longevity of Çatal Hüyük evidence of time before war and violence in human relations.[8]

Whether we can class Zuntz as a "feminist interpreter" or not is unimportant, as communion with the dead most certainly appears to have taken place in Çatal Hüyük.

***

Does this sense of renewal, or continuity, signify a belief in life after death? Certainly Eliade does not find this unlikely.[9] Once more the details offered by Eliade provide us with reasons for believing that there may have been belief in an afterlife. But the qualities on which I wish to focus at this point are the qualities of τερριβιλιτά by which death is often signified, and to do this we must look at the duality present in all matter.[10] Life and death are primary pairs of opposites as are male and female. This is the logic behind which the notion of duality itself is associated with the feminine. Since the opposite of creation is destruction, because the female is associated with creation then logically it

---

[7] Op. cit., 14, n.3.

[8] Radford Ruether, *Goddesses and the Divine Feminine*, op. cit., 29.

[9] Eliade, *A History of Religious Ideas*, op. cit., i., 10:

To sum up, we may conclude that the burials confirm the belief in survival (already indicated by the use of red ocher) and furnish some additional details: burials oriented toward the East, showing an intention to connect the fate of the soul with the course of the sun, hence the hope of a rebirth, that is, of a postexistence in another world; belief in the continuation of a specific activity; certain funeral rites, indicated by offerings of objects of personal adornment and by the remains of meals.

[10] Gimbutas, op. cit., 163:

The beginning of the concept of continuous life/death duality and of divine ambivalence as expressed in ancient Greek mythical images such as Hekate-Artemis, Demeter-Kore or Persephone, goes back to the Neolithic-Chalcolithic.

follows that the female must be associated with death and destruction. Any living person must reconcile with this most paramount duality. Bruce Lincoln describes a Proto-Indo-European (P-I-E) goddess, known as *Kolyo. *Kolyo represents both youth and beauty from her frontal view, but her back view represents the decomposition and decay of the grave.[11] She is the opposition of beauty and life to death and decay contained within the one symbolic figure. For Lincoln, this contrast is, at best, unpleasant and symbolizes the abyss which death represents to modern man. To say that this is so for the Proto-Indo-Europeans is an assumption. The presentation of opposites is just that—life and beauty contrast with death and decay. Let us consider *Kolyo and compare her to the description of The Loathly Bride, Lady or Lady Transformed in Coomaraswamy's essay "On the Loathly Bride."

> The correct interpretation is, no doubt, the one that is given by R.S. Loomis, who identifies her with the Earth Goddess and therefore with the Sovereignty—the kingdom, the power, and the glory which he who possesses the Earth enjoys.[12]

She, the Loathly Bride, represents the power of life and the knowledge of death. She is the soul of the world and each individual within that world. Through her, the soul possesses the Earth, but always with the knowledge that this must decay. The embrace of the Loathly Bride by the King, or King-to-be, empowers him and provides through her, dominion, the ability to rule: "Dominion; not the Ruler himself, but the Power, the Glory and the Fortune with which he operates."[13] In the first section on Blake we looked at the embrace of the other by Los, an embrace that is only able to take place when the gates of Enitharmon's heart open. When this embrace takes place, then the mortal world becomes the shadow world and not the world after death which Lincoln finds so frightening:

[11] Bruce Lincoln, *Death, War, and Sacrifice*, 1991, Chicago, University of Chicago Press, 15.

[12] Coomaraswamy, *Traditional Art and Symbolism*, op. cit., 353.

[13] Ibid., 357.

I already feel a World within,
Opening its gates, & in it all the real substances
Of which these in the outward World are shadows which
pass away.[14]

This may well have been the same for the Proto Indo Europeans
with their portrayal of *Kolyo. It is certainly true for the Vedic
and Tantric tradition: "In relation to the three functions of creation, preservation and destruction, Shakti is Sarasvati, Lakshmi
and Kālī."[15] The third element of the feminine in this tradition is
Kālī, the Black Goddess: "Kālī appears first as Sleep . . . "then as
Night and as a dream, and finally as Death herself."[16] "Creation,
preservation and destruction" are the three elements that make
up the feminine aspect, the soul of the human being, and are
repeated in the masculine spirit by Brahma, Vishnu, and Shiva.
The embrace of the Spirit by the Soul is what makes the wheels
of the universe turn.

But the belief in an afterlife, for our early ancestors, is something about which Lincoln is less sanguine.[17] Lincoln states that
all that is offered is "nothingness." That there is no notion that
this is salvific or can be avoided by way of bargaining, redemption, or any other means. Lincoln's argument is that life after
death is privative, without anything, and echoes the fate ordained
for Menelaus after death:

> But for yourself, Menelaus, fostered by Zeus, it is not
> ordained that you should die and meet your fate in horse-
> pasturing Argos, but to the Elysian plains and the ends of
> the earth will the immortals convey you, where dwells fair-
> haired Rhadamanthus, and where life is easiest for men. No
> snow is there, nor heavy storm, nor ever rain, but always

---

[14] K. 329, FZ. 7 : 364.

[15] Sivananda and Satyananda Saraswati, op. cit., 13.

[16] Wendy Doniger, trans. *Hindu Myths*, 1975, London, Penguin Books, 205–206.

[17] Lincoln, op. cit., 15:

That nothingness was the expectation is clear from the P-I-E formulaic description of the otherworld as a realm "without summer, without winter; without
heat, without cold; without suffering, without labor; without hunger, without
thirst; without illness, old age or death.

Ocean sends up blasts of the shrill-blowing West wind that they may give cooling to men; for you have Helen to wife, and are in their eyes the husband of the daughter of Zeus.[18]

Would Lincoln find what is offered to Menelaus as privative as the formula of the Proto-Indo-European? Menelaus, son-in-law of Zeus, is only promised fair weather. But to describe that as "nothingness" may be illogical and mistaken. This world cannot express what may be in the otherworld, and therefore it is more accurate to say merely what it is not. What it does give us is the knowledge that they believed in an otherworld. Or, perhaps a belief in the otherworld may be indicative of weakness and folly, as Hans Blumemberg claims, quoting Feuerbach. For Feuerbach, mankind invented and retained this myth through fear and what might be seen as a misplaced value of man's importance.[19] This argument places divinity in the "use only when needed" category, something that is removed whenever man decides, and is therefore only a human construct. For Feuerbach, the divinity is thus only a glorification of man. The replacement of a divine power by a secular power may best be exemplified by Marx's system.[20] The Marxian view sees religion as an agent that both shapes and reflects society. It is therefore easily replaced by a social power that does not elevate itself to the heavens but keeps most surely located within the material world.

Blumemberg's second main theory of religion

---

[18] Homer, *Odyssey*, trans. Murray, rev. Dimock, 2002, Cambridge, MA, Harvard University Press, 159–161, IV: 561–569. Hereafter citations from the *Odyssey* will be shown in the text as follows: *Od. IV*: 561–569.

[19] Hans Blumemberg, *Work on Myth*, trans. Wallace, 1985, Cambridge, MA, MIT Press, 28:

[The] divinity is nothing but man's self-projection into heaven, his temporary representation in a foreign medium, through which his self-concept is enriched and becomes capable of retraction from its interim state of projection.

[20] Bowker, op. cit., 11:

Where Feuerbach had glimpsed the way in which God is constructed as a projection of the ideals that humans hold of themselves at their best, Marx realized that the projection is never individual but always social. It arises in what we now call "the social construction of knowledge"; and *as* projection, it reflects, expresses and perpetuates existing social and economic relationships.

is represented by Rudolf Otto, for whom God and the gods arise from an *a priori* and homogeneous original sensation of the "holy," in which awe and fear, fascination and world anxiety, uncanniness and unfamiliarity are secondarily combined.[21]

Otto's idea of the "numinous" imbues every person and thing with holiness. It has much in common with that of the Oglala Lakota in their Sacred Pipe prayer.

> My relatives, Grandmother and Mother Earth, we are of earth, and belong to You. O Mother Earth from whom we receive our food, You care for our growth as do our own mothers. Every step that we take upon You should be done in a sacred manner; each step should be as a prayer. Remember this my relatives: that the power of this pure soul will be with you as you walk, for it, too, is the fruit of Mother Earth; it is as a seed, planted in your center, which will in time grow in your hearts, and cause our generations to walk in a *wakan* manner.[22]

To dismiss this as animistic would be incorrect. The "pure soul ... planted in your center," Blake's "centre of sweet delight," imbues life with holiness, with the idea of the numinous. Blumemberg is more closely aligned with the Marxian view that religion is a myth purveyed by the ruling class which, by means of fear, controls and suppresses any reaction to the social environment inhabited by its followers.

Bowker repudiates this view of the myth of immortal life.

> It becomes clear, therefore, that the material collected by anthropologists cannot be claimed to support the view that the human consciousness of death led to the invention of religion, as a compensation for the fear which that consciousness evokes.[23]

For Bowker it is not fear that enables man to put together a fairy story to help them die in peace. If it is not fear that causes the

[21] Blumemberg, op. cit., 8.
[22] Brown, op. cit., 13.
[23] Bowker, op. cit., 23.

creation of the myth, or the need to control the masses, then what does drive humanity in the search for a spiritual, or other-worldly, meaning to their existence? For it may be presumptive to state, as Lincoln does, that all humans "recoil from nothingness . . . as their ends draw near. We may contrast this with Zuntz's description of the Rock Graves in Pantalica, Sicily:

> Death resides in this immense stone; at the same time, it is vibrating with the potency of unquenchable life. Enter any one of the graves; you feel, as nowhere else, that you are in the womb of the Great Mother, from which the dead will be reborn, mysteriously, for another span in the light above.[24]

Here death is potent, linked with the power of the womb, and signalling the possibility of birth and rebirth. Does this make our modern rational world poorer by our non-acceptance of death? For many in the modern world Richard Jeffries' idea of the soul and spirit is as good as it gets:

> That there is no knowing, in the sense of written reasons, whether the soul lives on or not, I am fully aware. I do not hope or fear. At least while I am living I have enjoyed the idea of immortality, and the idea of my own soul. If then, after death, I am resolved without exception into earth, air, and water, and the spirit goes out like a flame, still I shall have had the glory of that thought.[25]

The world Jeffries knew and loved was being changed apace by the rapid growth of industrialism in England. Since that time our world has become even less glorious. That we should have even "the glory of that thought," and that this is something we share with our predecessors, has been lost for many moderns. Contemporary means of coping with death in our society are many and various, although not always clearly designated. It is not written that one should wear black clothes, or white, or red, in honor of the deceased for a period of so many days. It is not written that one should scar one's cheeks, or breast, or shave one's head. Rather than a demonstration of how we might feel in reaction to

---

[24] Zuntz, op. cit., 62.

[25] Richard Jefferies, *The Story of My Heart*, 1947, London, Constable, 39.

loss, we are urged to "soldier on," to disguise any pain or sorrow. To survive this period of loss we must for the most part do so without the use of rituals. The removal of rituals to help acknowledge loss may well leave the person more bereft. Where do we honor our dead and feel the potency of their having lived except within us? Far from being a potent force, death nowadays makes us feel impotent. In a society that prides itself upon learning the answer to any problem, the impotency caused by death—and society's inability to deny death its victory—seeks instead to pretend that it just doesn't happen. That this puts contemporary society at odds with those that have preceded it is obvious. To rely upon mechanistic science is even more of a nullity than the nothingness Lincoln claimed was faced by our earliest ancestors. It is no longer death that is the nothingness, but life itself.

Let us look at the argument Socrates puts forward for regarding death with equanimity in *The Phaedo*.

> This then is why a man should be of good cheer about his soul, who in his life has rejected the pleasures and ornaments of the body, thinking they are alien to him and more likely to do him harm than good, and has sought eagerly for those of learning, and after adorning his soul with no alien ornaments, but with its own proper adornment of self-restraint and justice and courage and freedom and truth, awaits his departure to the other world, ready to go when fate calls him.[26]

By casting away the values of the material world, the soul/spirit is able to seek out those intangible ideals that will allow man properly to regard his own death as a progression to a higher state. Modern society tends to conceal the fact that death has occurred. We pick up where we left off before the event, returning to our work situation, even starting another relationship, continuing with our life as if nothing has happened, perhaps allowing mem-

[26] Plato, *The Phaedo*, trans. Fowler, 2001, Cambridge, Harvard University Press, 390–393:

The tripartite soul, ψυχή, of Plato allows for the soul to possess immutability. This is as Blake's spirit.

ories to intrude in the still silent moments when the world does not impinge upon us. But memories remain with us for a reason. Not just the memories of the physical characteristics or activities of those dead, but the memories of how the interrelationship of human activity took place and how that links with what may or may not follow. In Bruce Lincoln's article "Waters of Memory, Waters of Forgetfulness," he traces the most frequent Indo-European versions about the after-world that concern crossing water. Through a reading of the various versions he arrives at the following conclusions. After death and while crossing the water to the other world, the memories are washed away and carried by the river to a spring where they "were drunk by certain highly favored individuals, who became inspired and infused with supernatural wisdom."[27] Early Indo-European families arrived at an acceptance of death that presupposed there was a more profound reason for living. That reason allowed them to live their lives in a manner which prepared them for death and after-death.[28] True wisdom allows for the knowledge that those who die will contribute to the life of those who survive them by enabling them to cope, or indeed to take joy in the knowledge that this is the purpose of life. That it is not just surviving in the material world which is of importance because this life inevitably leads to death, and then perhaps to the other world where we in turn contribute

[27] Lincoln, op. cit., 57:

For on the one hand, the otherworld is quite often cut off from this one; the soul making the passage must leave behind all his memories, all the history he has accumulated during his life. But on the other, this world is not cut off from the next in the same sense, for those memories constantly flow back and become a source of the deepest wisdom and most profound inspiration.

[28] Ibid., 58:

But the memories of the departed are not without value for those who are yet living. The accumulated memories of the dead comprise the totality of human history. Preserved and appreciated, they are the source of true wisdom, the wisdom that is based on the full sweep of human experience rather than just the idiosyncratic events of one human life. In the last analysis, the present depends upon the past, the living upon the dead, and this world upon the other. Those who die do not just pass on but continue to contribute to the sustenance of this world, as the world of the living draws strength, meaning, and wisdom from the world of the dead, much as one draws water from a spring.

to the sum of knowledge. The knowledge that comes from the stream of memories may slake some thirst for wisdom. To deny this by ignoring death, as Western society tends to do, is to deny ourselves access to wisdom. Just as birth is an event to be received with joy, death is also something that must be acknowledged as a means of growth. Socrates tells his companions that "after I have drunk the poison I shall no longer be with you, but shall go away to the joys of the blessed."[29] For Socrates there is no fear that this will not be so, and nor was there for Blake. In Alexander Gilchrist's *Life of William Blake* we are able to read of his last days in the chapter so named:

> The final leave-taking came he had so often seen in vision; so often, and with such childlike, simple faith, sung and designed. *The Death of the Good Old Man,* he enacted it— serenely, joyously. For life and design and song were with him all pitched in one key, different expressions of one reality. No dissonances there![30]

Blake shared with Socrates the belief that this world is merely a gateway to the otherworld so despairingly named by Lincoln as nothingness. We are told that on the day of his death "he composed and uttered songs to his Maker so sweetly to the ear of his Catherine" and disclaimed ownership of these paeans. He told Catherine that "they would not be parted; he should always be about her to take care of her."[31] Both Socrates and Blake are representative of our culture as it has evolved over centuries. Through them we are also linked back to the potency of death, described by Zuntz, in the Rock Caves of Sicily, which are symbolic of the womb and may thereby signify rebirth, a rebirth that is not material but linked with this materiality because that is what is known.

[29] Plato, *The Phaedo,* trans. Fowler, op. cit., 394–395.
[30] Gilchrist, op. cit., 352.
[31] Ibid.

PART THREE

Woman and Goddess
in Archaic Greece

5

The Goddess, Woman, and Marriage in the *Iliad*

THE *Iliad* is ostensibly about the recovery of a wayward wife. That Troy, or Ilium, was extremely rich may also have contributed to this ten-year siege. Until the commencement of this tale, those captured, from either side, were able to ransom their release, and all appeared content with this arrangement, except perhaps for the lower ranks, as shown by Thersites' minor rebellion. The dramatic change that occurs is the story of the *Iliad* and concerns the possession and loss of another woman.

The *Iliad* is one of our greatest Western myths, and it could be called a tragedy—but this is too limiting a definition. Tragedy is a necessary opposite to the comic or joyful side of life; death is a necessary correlative to life. H.D.F. Kitto defines the Greek attitude to tragedy as habitual.[1] He then qualifies this "tragic turn of thought" by demonstrating their zest for life.[2] Kitto argues that this is not just resignation—a resignation he finds in the Judaic outlook—nor the resigned acceptance of the Chinese, but a delight in man and his capabilities tempered by the knowledge that this too must pass. This does appear to relate closely to the potency of death described by Zuntz.

It is possible to read the *Iliad* as a book about the perceived masculine attributes of fighting, posturing in game-cock fashion, demonstrating pride in physical attributes, loyalty to one's brother before all else. Perhaps it is a tragedy that these male virtues are stressed. But these were the virtues of Classical Greece.

[1] H.D.F. Kitto, *The Greeks*, 1974, Middlesex, Penguin Books, 59.
[2] Ibid., 61.

Kitto demonstrates this with the passage concerning Hector and Andromache, one which

> gives us a glimpse into the very soul of the Homeric hero. What moves him to deeds of heroism is not a sense of duty as we understand it—duty towards others: it is rather duty towards himself. He strives after that which we translate "virtue," but is in Greek *arete*, "excellence."[3]

This pursuit towards excellence is not undertaken with the promise of a great reward after death: the realization of excellence in any task undertaken, particularly a heroic one, is itself the reward. The *Odyssey*, however, is a love story with a "successful" conclusion. More importantly, when taken together, the *Iliad* and the *Odyssey*—which are the foundation of our Western mythic literature—represent the virtues and shortcomings of both male and female.

The question of whether the mother Goddess of pre-history can be found in this, our first written record, remains. We encounter Demeter, the Greek Mother Goddess, in the *Iliad*, a mere five times. Her first mention is in Book II, where her precinct is described.[4] Then, in one of Homer's beautiful similes, he describes the fighting between the Achaeans and the Argives after Sarpedon rouses Hector with stinging words. The wheeling chariots and the men raise a dust such as is raised when the winnowing takes place in the threshing room.

> And just as the wind carries chaff about the holy threshing floors of men that are winnowing, when golden-haired

[3] Ibid., 59. Liddell & Scott, *Greek-English Lexicon*, 1987, Oxford, OUP, define this characteristic as follows are ἀρετή:

goodness, excellence, of any kind: but in Homer, like Lat *virtus* (from *vir*), *manhood, prowess, valor:* also *manly beauty, dignity,* etc. 2. in Prose, of the *virtues* of land, fountains, etc. 3. *excellence in art or workmanship,* skill. II. in moral sense, *goodness, virtue:*—also *character for virtue, reputation, merit.*

[4] Homer, *Iliad*, trans. Murray, rev: Wyatt, 1999, Cambridge, Mass. Harvard University Press. Hereafter citations will be shown by Book Number followed by Line Number as follows: *II:II:695–96.* I have used the Murray translation throughout the work, unless otherwise stated, because I find it less inflammatory than some others.

Demeter among the driving blasts of wind separates the grain from the chaff.[5]

Demeter is clearly a grain goddess, but she is not the "Moon Goddess, product of a sedentary, matrilinear community, encompassing the archetypal unity and multiplicity of feminine nature," as described by Gimbutas and which she felt went with settlement and farming. Demeter is insignificant in the *Iliad*, and the other mentions of her are minor. What is interesting is the mention of Demeter among the list of women and goddesses bedded by Zeus who have roused him to sexual desire. Only Leto and Demeter do not have progeny listed from their union.[6] Persephone, who is Demeter's daughter in the *Homeric Hymn to Demeter*, is mentioned only twice in the *Iliad*. On both occasions she is linked with the underworld and given the epithet ἐπαινή, "dread," "exceedingly awful."[7] That Demeter is a mother and that her daughter is Persephone have no importance in the *Iliad*. Kitto's explanation is that Greek-speaking peoples gradually took over the non-Hellenic race that was indigenous to Attica and the Peloponnese.[8] Thus the Greek speakers, who infiltrated rather than invaded the land, brought the language to the original inhabitants, and Kitto names them the Achaeans. The *Iliad* is their story. The Pelasgians, in particular the Athenians, claim to be the oldest inhabitants of Greece, and Kitto makes a very important point when he tells us that they were worshippers of female goddesses, in particular in Argos and Athens, Athena and Argive Hera.[9] There is, therefore, an uneasy alliance between these nature goddesses and the mainly male gods of the Achaeans. It will be necessary, therefore, to look elsewhere in this poem for indications concerning the role of the feminine.

The passivity of the feminine, in the *Iliad*, allows the masculine

---

[5] Further references to Demeter are as follows: *Il. V*:499–501, *XIII*:322, *XIV*:326, *XXI*:76.

[6] *Il. XIV*:326: "Though Zeus acts as father when Persephone is bidden to marry Hades."

[7] *Il. IX*:457, *Il. IX*:568–569.

[8] Kitto, op. cit., 15.

[9] Ibid., 18.

to be unbridled. That is not to say that the female could necessarily have done otherwise, short of adopting Lysistrata's remedy. But Homer shows very clearly what occurs when one sex is dominant. No one wins, although, later, Helen is recaptured and Menelaus takes possession of his wife once more. Later, too, the grandiosity of Agamemnon is rewarded with death, one foreseen by his captured prize, Cassandra, another powerless female. The *Iliad* is about the wrath of Achilles, although, almost by chance, it also involves the recovery of Helen, the wife of Menelaus. Achilles' wrath is roused by Agamemnon, the leader of the team in pursuit, when his prize, Briseis, is taken in replacement for the prize of Agamemnon, Chryseis. Remember, these are the first two women we meet in the *Iliad*. As Agamemnon is the leader of the attacking force, he sees it as his right to lay claim to the best prizes taken in capture, because this reflects upon his ἀρετή. He forfeits his right to Chryseis because he had spurned the application of Chryses—her father and a priest of Apollo—for her return, an act of impiety. Apollo intervenes, the Argives are punished, and Agamemnon has to pay tribute to Chryses, part of which is the return of his daughter.

The *Iliad* is a cautionary tale as it proceeds to demonstrate just what occurs when men and gods do not control their desires. Greed, wrongful pride, anger, lust, and uncontrolled actions during battle are all punished. For the Trojans this is soon to result in the complete destruction of their city and way of life. It is of no consequence that Athene was the goddess to whom the women of Ilium paid homage, nor does it help the Trojans that they continue to demonstrate their belief in her throughout the war. She turns her back on her city although she is named as a polis goddess, and Ilium was above all a polis. The Trojans are represented as being effete when compared with the Greek force attacking them. Sybaritic, with the exception of Hector, seducers of other men's wives, untrustworthy, breakers of the code of behavior that governs guests, and, particularly in Paris' case, unable to stand up and fight for the woman he supposedly loves. Nevertheless the Trojans are the most clearly-defined representatives of the family unit.

The anger of Achilles, provoked by Agamemnon's greed and arrogant pride, causes the death of many more Greeks. Peter

Rose sees this as a power struggle between meritocracy and plutocracy.[10] This may well be the case, but whether this is a power
struggle or not, the end result is the same, and Homer tells us that
both protagonists are ultimately dead. We do not hear from
Briseis again until Book XIX, and her sad little lament echoes the
sadness of her life.[11] This woman is prepared to marry the man
who has been part of the killing of her father and brothers. Their
town has been razed to the ground. In order to achieve protection
she is willing, even eager, to marry the hero who has done these
things. Her prospective bridegroom, who says his anger towards
Agamemnon is caused by the fact that he truly loves her, was to
be urged into marrying her by his best friend, and she mourns the
loss of a kindly advocate. Briseis will be unprotected after the
death of Achilles until someone else takes over. We may contrast
her relationship with Achilles to the response of Priam when he
asks Achilles for the body of his son. Achilles, whose anger has
caused the death of his dearest friend, Patroclus, and whose desire
for eternal fame will change Briseis' future, releases Hector's
body to Priam that he may be buried with full funeral rites, something that will not occur for Priam himself. With the assistance of
Hermes, Priam reaches the tent of Achilles,

> and, coming up to Achilles, clasped his knees in his hands,
> and kissed his hands, the terrible, man-slaying hands that
> had slain his many sons.[12]

Priam's speech to Achilles, states that he has

> endured what no other mortal on the face of the earth has
> yet endured, to reach out my hand to the face of the man
> who has slain my son.[13]

There is an undertone of horror that this is what he has done.
Women, on the other hand, make "love" to those who have killed
their loved ones and no horror is expressed. Briseis is still sleeping

---

[10] Peter W. Rose, *Sons of the Gods, Children of the Earth*, 1992, New York, Cor-
nell University Press.

[11] *Il. XIX*: 287–300.

[12] *Il. XXIV*: 477–479.

[13] Ibid., 505–506.

in Achilles' bed. Very clearly, at this point and just in case we have missed it elsewhere, we are shown the relegation of the female in the *Iliad*. The polis goddesses, as Kitto has named them and the sex they represent, are dismissed. Women are subservient in this warlike culture and are clearly shown to be so in this poem as they perform the necessary manoeuvres to maintain their positions.

Again, in passing, Homer presents us with many pictures of the heroes consoling themselves, after a hard day fighting, with the pleasures of the female. After Achilles has lost Briseis to Agamemnon, we meet Diomede and Iphis accompanying Achilles and Patroclus on their couches.[14] Diomede is the substitute, the reserve squeeze, for Briseis now that Agamemnon has claimed her. Expanding this picture glimpsed so briefly we may imagine that all over the plains of Ilium, where the forces are camped, there are men in bed with women if they have fought bravely enough to warrant a prize. This is masculine pride at its very best. A strong arm, a stout heart, and all chaps together. Even Nestor, described by Homer as "the old charioteer," has his companion to comfort him after a hard day driving the horses.[15] What follows from this elevation of purely male traits is the derogation of female traits. Woman, "she," becomes an object, at best an object who is aware of the likelihood of her fate; at worst, unnamed and unmentioned. There is little trace of reverence for the mother goddess here. Helen is condemned by her beauty to be a thing, and promised as a reward to Paris for his choice of Aphrodite in the most beautiful goddess award. This award brings Athene, Aphrodite, and Hera into contest. I do not think that it matters greatly that this is thought by some commentators to be interpolation. Indeed, if this simplified judgement based purely on physical beauty—with no thought or mention of anything moral, emotional, or intelligent contained within a beautiful shell—is seen as a means of explanation for what occurs, then perhaps it deserves to have as its end the Trojan War. There are other reasons for the war to have taken place, even one as simple as Paris's behavior as a guest in Menelaus's home. And we can quite reason-

---

[14] *Il. IX*:663–668.
[15] *Il. XI*:624–626.

ably assume that Ilium was so wealthy that there would be much to be shared between the victors. It is unlikely that any war has ever been fought without an accompanying justification that tends to disguise the real reason for the war.

Whether she is the prize promised to Paris by Aphrodite or she is a wanton woman who has chosen to mate with a beautiful man, Helen's physical self has cost her any chance of an ordinary life, and when we first meet her she is shown as filled with longing for her home. Is this feeling genuine? Maybe, if the first reason for her being there is the fault of the goddess. Humans are given various gifts by various gods. For Helen, it was her beauty and, as the Chinese say, "Beauty has a thin fate." As Paris is a recipient of Aphrodite's gifts, he is a pleasure-seeking, randy little cockscomb and he praises the "sweet desire" bestowed by Aphrodite. He doesn't object to donning the plumage that is part of the warlike male of this time, but he does object to being physically damaged. Paris' physical expertise is at its best in the bedroom, and it is to the bedroom that Aphrodite whisks him when he looks as if his wares might be damaged by Menelaus. Aphrodite, the goddess who supports the Trojans perhaps as much because she has caused the problems that beset them as for any other reason, intercedes on behalf of Paris. He is Aphrodite's plaything as much as Helen is his. So, the humans plot and promise, but the gods say "not yet." Although Helen scorns Paris for his cowardice, after his escape from the duel with Menelaus her fate or her desire is to climb into bed with him while confusion reigns outside the walls of Troy. Menelaus strides up and down, searching for Paris while Paris is enjoying a mid-afternoon romp with Helen. This is the terrible destiny of this poem. How does one describe this moment of passion that takes place while the husband is looking for the guilty party? I think it is obviously meant to be funny. There is the cuckolded husband, breathing smoke through his nostrils, as he strides through the dust looking for the person responsible for his shame while he, the cuckolder, is enjoying himself in the comfort of his chambers with the wife, after the complete debacle at the cuckold's hands on the battlefield. Is it love or lust? Or, perhaps a little light relief from the dreadful scenes of battle? Maybe this touches all the male listeners or readers at a point where they are most vulnerable, and a laugh at someone else's fate may ease the tension of their own.

When Helen describes herself and her relationship to those below the walls of Troy to Priam, "And he was husband's brother to shameless me, if ever there was such a one."[16] This is the A. T. Murray translation of the word κυνώπισος, "shameless."[17] There are other more subjective translations. Richmond Lattimore's 1951 translation uses the phrase "slut that I am,"[18] Martin Hammond's interpretation, in 1987, "whore that I am,"[19] and Robert Fagles' translation, in 1990, "whore that I am!"[20] These particular self-deprecatory remarks spoken by Helen, both here and in Book VI, seem to rouse some translators' ire. Fagles softens his tone for the second use of the same word by Helen, when she is speaking to Hector: "My dear brother, dear to me, bitch that I am, vicious, scheming—horror to freeze the heart!"[21] As does Hammond: "My brother—brother of the bitch, the scheming, horrible creature that I am!"[22] In contrast, Lattimore is quite gentlemanly: "Brother by marriage to me, who am a nasty bitch evil-intriguing."[23] It appears that contemporary translators have more problems with Helen than does the one man who stands to lose everything, and indeed does: "you are in no way to blame in my eyes; it is the gods, surely who are to blame."[24] Priam has absolved her of blame and acknowledges the same forces of destiny that operate on him also operate on her. Her words, spoken to Hector who has arrived to urge Paris to fight, "O brother of

[16] *Il. III*:179.

[17] Liddell & Scott, op. cit.: κυνώη, οὐ, ὁ ("the dog-eyed, i.e., shameless one: —fem., κυνωῆι, ιδό, ἡ), the shameless woman; also fierce-eyed, terrible."

[18] Homer, *The Iliad of Homer,* trans. Lattimore, 1961, Chicago and London, The University of Chicago Press.

[19] Homer, *The Iliad,* trans. Hammond, 1987, Middlesex, Penguin Books.

[20] Homer, *The Iliad,* trans. Fagles, intro. Knox, 1997, Bath, England, The Softback Preview.

[21] *Il. VI*:344.

[22] Ibid.

[23] Ibid.

[24] *Il. III*:164.

me that am a dog, a contriver of mischief and abhorred by all,"[25] are harsh. But I would very much doubt that she would call herself "whore." I would certainly say that she is manipulative. By describing herself in this manner she is pre-empting criticism. Both Priam and Hector are kind to her. But do these words make her actions worse? She demonstrates a level of awareness about her situation which Paris does not share. Is this an attempt to shift blame onto the female? Or is it Homer demonstrating that a beautiful package does not necessarily contain anything of worth? But we need to remember that there were two beautiful packages, Helen and Paris, both of whom considered the "world well lost to love." It would seem that some translators prefer to lay the blame on Helen, although anyone reading the *Iliad* would be struck by just how little choice these women had to alter their destiny. One must take into account that it is not only the Greeks who have problems with women. So do some contemporary translators. I have no particular brief for Helen, and we must remember the other half of this liaison, Paris, who is after all merely a bowman. A pretty man who loves a pretty woman, or at least lusts after her—and, after all, it takes a couple to copulate.

Empty-headed, vain Paris, with all his accoutrements of military might, plays at manhood, but his brother Hector is a man. A man who has "learnt to fight among the foremost Trojans, striving to win great glory for my father and myself."[26] Hector alone "guarded Ilios."[27] Hector is clearly aware of what his wife Andromache's fate will be if Troy is taken, and prays that he will be dead before he hears her cries as she is taken away. This prayer is granted him, but not the prayer for his son, Astyanax. Despite this awareness, Hector pursues his fate:

> Dear wife, in no way, I beg you, grieve excessively at heart for me; no man beyond what is fated shall send me to Hades; but his fate, say I, no man has ever escaped, whether he is base or noble, when once he has been born.[28]

[25] *Il.VI*:344.
[26] Ibid., 445–446.
[27] Ibid., 403.
[28] Ibid., 486–489.

Hector has no other choice than to follow his fate, to be Troy's defense, to bring glory to his father, and to protect his brother— pretentious Paris. Bernard Knox describes him with sympathy, as we know Zeus has decided the result of this war and that this "protector of the polis" will be defeated.[29] Hector's role as defender means that he must sacrifice his role as husband. Knox makes a very clear distinction between the killing machine, Achilles, and a man who is more accustomed to fighting in defence of his city. Indeed, until the death of Patroclus, Trojans who were beaten on the battlefield had been able to ransom their freedom from the Achaeans, thus enriching Greek coffers and not putting too deadly a countenance upon this war. As Knox says, they were fighting a civilized war.[30]

Hector is a product of this civilized city, and he shows indecision when it comes to the final battle between himself and Achilles. The choice of protecting his wife and son by sacrificing Paris, which does not occur to him until too late, may well have seemed a much better alternative. Like Achilles, he chooses glory, ἀρετή. Paris is despised by Hector and the other Trojans for his lack of martial commitment, but he is not handed over with Helen to the Achaeans. Hector meets his fate alone, and he is beaten by a man who is full of "raw, self-absorbed fury."[31]

The most clearly-defined human woman is Andromache, the wife of Hector. She personifies the maternal and wifely virtues, love for her husband and child; she pays honor to the goddess of the city, but it is to no avail. Hector is forecasting her future clearly when he speaks of possible outcomes if they are defeated by the Achaeans. A very bleak future it is for her and their son, Astyanax. Unlike Helen, Andromache is not held to her position by the influence of a goddess unless we see her as representing the maternal virtues befitting a follower of the Mother Goddess, but this is not clear. She does not run away nor is she compelled to stay as is Helen. Instead, she obeys the commands of her husband and retires to her home to pursue her wifely tasks in a

[29] Knox, *Iliad*, Introduction and Notes, op. cit., 34.
[30] Ibid., 32.
[31] Ibid., 56.

proper manner. Her reward is slavery. The end result for Andromache, Briseis, Diomede, Iphis, and all the other unnamed
women clearly defines what is wrong with the masculine choices
as far as the female sex is concerned. Helen argues with Aphrodite when told to entertain Paris, but she is unable to resist the
passion, lust or love, when ordered to submit. Andromache is not
able to sway her husband to hold to the feminine values of home
and family against the warlike values of both Trojans and Greeks.
Even when Andromache begs Hector not to fight alone outside
the walls, it is to no avail. Neither woman is able to change or
improve their situation. One woman is shown as successful in her
demands. Hecuba, who, distressed at Priam's intent to retrieve
the body of their son Hector, insists that Priam make a libation to
Zeus asking for a sign that he will be safe. Priam acquiesces, Zeus
sends an eagle, and a female has demanded something of a male
successfully.[32] But this is a hollow success. Hecuba and Priam,
rulers of Troy, will be defeated by the Greeks after the mourning
period for Hector. Allowing the masculine values to run rampant, as Johnson states, is a "flaw in man."[33]

Possibly the most rampant male is Achilles, and later we read
how he feels he has paid the price for this in the *Odyssey*. In Book
IX of the *Iliad*, Achilles describes his two fates:

> For my mother the goddess, silver-footed Thetis, tells me
> that twofold fates are bearing me toward the doom of death:
> if I remain here and fight about the city of the Trojans, then
> lost is my return home, but my renown will be imperish-
> able; but if I return home to my dear native land, lost then is
> my glorious renown, yet will my life long endure, and the
> doom of death will not come soon on me.[34]

---

[32] *Il. XXIV*:283–321.

[33] Johnson, op. cit., 44:

fatal unless he wakens to it—that he carefully arranges life so that the feminine
will pay the price for his masculine creation. . . . Worst of all, because it is so sub-
tle, he may take the high stuff of consciousness and leave the feminine within
himself to pay the price: inner darkness and meaninglessness.

[34] *Il. IX*:410–416.

At this point in the tale Achilles has refused the generous induce-
ments offered by Agamemnon for him to return to the battle. He
has not decided which fate he will choose, and in the end it is a
conscious choice he makes for pride and glory, masculine values,
rather than the choice of home and family, feminine values. This
choice is also made from brotherly love, not unlike the "mate-
ship" demonstrated in early Australian literature, when, in Book
XVI, Patroclus is killed. The order of importance given to these
traits appears to be pride, glory, honor to one's father, and love
for one's brother.

The honor promised by Achilles to the dead Patroclus, apart
from the "head of Hector," is a lament by Trojan and Dardanian
women that entails also their shedding of tears.[35] The women
may well weep, but not for the death of Patroclus. It will be for
the death of their sons, husbands, fathers, and freedom. Hecuba
and Priam grieve for the loss of their greatest son, Hector, and
Andromache for the loss of her child's father. This is the true
price of this Trojan War. Fatherless children, husbandless wives,
childless parents, condemned to slavery or death, and the "work
of women's hands" incinerated. The masculine search for glory
results in annihilation of all that is held dear by the feminine.
Now Achilles is able to farewell his friend, Patroclus, as he drags
home Hector's body to join the corpse of his dead friend. Patroclus is burned, in company with twelve Trojans, the odd horse
and dog, and with the corpse of Hector beside his pyre. After this
event of mourning the funeral games are held. The first prize for
the chariot race, along with a tripod, is "a woman to lead away,
one skilled in noble handiwork."[36] "Skilled in noble handiwork"
may be her defining attribute but she is unnamed and only one of
the prizes given away. Knox makes the point that Achilles is a different man here, as host of the games, that he

> is the great Achilles of the later aristocratic tradition, the
> man of princely courtesy and innate nobility visible in every
> aspect of his bearing and conduct, the Achilles who was
> raised by the centaur Chiron. It is a vision of what Achilles

[35] *Il. XVIII* : 339–342.
[36] Ibid., 263.

might have been in peace, if peace had been a possibility in the heroic world, or, for that matter, in Homer's world.[37]

Of course, that courtesy is not extended to the woman given as a prize. On Priam's return to Troy with the corpse of Hector, the grieving takes place. Andromache speaks first and with perception regarding the fate of herself and her son, weeping for the lost chance to remember Hector on his death bed. Hecuba weeps for her son, for Achilles has cost her many sons. Helen speaks last, "So I wail alike for you and for my unlucky self with grief at heart,"[38] as she remembers the gentleness of Hector and his protection of her. Hector's funeral pyre is the end of the *Iliad*. Men have met their glorious ends and will leave women grieving, stateless, and above all else in this poem, unacknowledged— except by Homer, who allows their lament to be the closing lines in the *Iliad*. Pity as an emotion—in particular, the Blakean transcendent pity—is not shown very often in this poem. Yet such is the skill of the poet that the audience is moved to pity for the losses these men and women incur through their actions.

If we rely only upon a reading of the *Iliad* as the basis for argument, women and women's virtues or strengths are treated as insignificant by the men who surround them. Yet Homer concludes the *Iliad* with three Trojan women mourning the loss of a husband, son, and friend. This is a very traditional role for women and one that does not change for many ages.[39] Can we expect the same treatment for the goddesses? In this epic battle

---

[37] Knox, *Iliad*, Introduction and Notes, op. cit., 57.

[38] *Il. XXIV*: 273.

[39] Helene P. Foley, *Female Acts in Greek Tragedy*, 2001, Princeton, Princeton University Press, 14:

Foley is discussing Greek society at the time of the Peloponnesian War, which lasted nearly thirty years. The public role of women's mourning begins to alter with the laws of Solon: "A society that aimed increasingly over the sixth and fifth centuries to preserve the individual household but subordinate it to the state needed to manage grief. But the privatizing of individual funerals and the self-controlled glorification of the war dead in Athenian public funerals did not necessarily leave enough room for the recognition of suffering and loss involved in individual deaths."

the Achaeans are supported by Hera and Athene and Aphrodite and Ares, with some help from Apollo, side with the Trojans.

I propose that along with the cautionary aspect, the *Iliad* is Homer's exposition of the loss of the goddess, Neumann's Great Mother. In this poem one sidedness, male and female, is clearly shown. Two parallel worlds exist: one male: fighting, strutting, wounding, drinking, winning, sharing a bed with the opposite sex; the other female: bathing, laving, cooking, tending, and sharing a bed with the opposite sex, which is as it should be and is a point of contact. But Homer's point of contact between male and female mortals, in the *Iliad* and particularly for the Greeks, is a purely physical one. There is no sacred union of opposites, no *hieros gamos*, none of Blake's "undivided essence." There is not even an acknowledgment, from the Greek camp, of the wonder of creating life, although when death overtakes them many of the heroes, Greek as well as Trojan, acknowledge that they have left behind a grieving wife and a child who will be fatherless. To some extent the Trojans acknowledge the existence of feminine characteristics. But, that is all. Does this make them worse because they are more fully able to see what they are to lose, unlike the Greeks who are so filled with the virtues of masculinity that there is no room for an acknowledgment of the feminine, let alone its loss?

Western European culture traces its ancestry back to the Greeks. They are our models. It is their iconography that we lay claim to, as devotees or destroyers.

> But European civilization was not created in the space of a few centuries; the roots are deeper—by six thousand years. That is to say, vestiges of the myths and artistic concepts of Old Europe, which endured from the seventh to the fourth millennium BC were transmitted to the modern Western world and became part of its cultural heritage.[40]

We may not be able to say that Bachofen's Mother Goddess, or Gimbutas' matrilineal or matrilocal goddesses, are clearly discernible, particularly in the *Iliad*. Traces of them remain, nevertheless,

[40] Gimbutas, op. cit., 238.

in this poem. The new reign of the Achaeans, which supplanted the older reign of the goddess who probably arrived with Cretan infiltration, was validated by the *Iliad*. Kitto has named Athene and Hera as major polis goddesses, and while these goddesses play important roles in the poem, their roles are tailored to suit the ethos of the new rule and to bring victory to the new gods.[41]

★ ★ ★

But Homer did create feminine heroes. The "successful" ones were the goddesses in the *Iliad*. It is true that the mortal women were "unsuccessful" in this poem, but Homer does not leave it there. In the *Iliad* the great heroes pursue purely masculine goals. Everything is subsumed in that desire to produce a heroic and glorious end to a male's life. But, again, women who believed in the value of their own lives and were listening to this story would have been singularly unimpressed. Although the worlds are parallel, one is predominant in this story. The dominance of the masculine in this work of Homer reflects the loss of recognition of the female, or more accurately, reflects the dominant beliefs of the culture about which the song was sung, at least in wartime.

But this dominance is less real than it seems. The recognition that had been accorded to the mother goddess in pre-history is not apparent, but is still there in the role of the female goddesses. I would argue that Bachofen's proposal that in the period known as pre-history society was ruled by females, and that matriarchy was in force before the patriarchal Greeks implanted their ideas upon future generations, is an unlikely one. Neumann's version of events is probably closer. Neumann's position is that the differences between the relative sizes and strengths of male and female in a culture that was dependent on physical strength make it unlikely that a female who was too weak to feed the tribe by killing a wild animal would be leader. This seems to be a far more realistic interpretation of the situation.[42] But, woman would be viewed with some degree of awe because of her ability to reproduce herself, seemingly unaided if the earlier Gimbutas is to be

[41] Kitto, op. cit., 18–19.
[42] Neumann, op. cit., 91.

91

believed.[43] Gimbutas's work on the goddess of Old Europe portrays her as androgynous and able to reproduce from herself. So while physically weaker, this creature—this softer, different, and mysterious being who has the potential to bring great pleasure to the opposite sex—also has the ability to ensure that the race survives. Obviously this must occur because something greater, stronger, infinitely more powerful than both male and female allows this to happen. The godhead, seen as feminine because of the then inexplicable potential for growth within the female, nevertheless still contains allusions to the masculine. That is, the masculine ability for growth, represented by the penis, which is included in some of the goddess sculptures as part of the feminine entity.

Neumann states "the woman contains and protects, nourishes and gives birth."[44] In short, the woman transforms matter from herself. Spinning, with its magical capacity for increase from what is less useful, is a natural symbol for the feminine. It is another representative example of producing something from nothing. In the penultimate Night of *The Four Zoas*, Blake allocates the attribute of spinning to the feminine counterpart of the Zoa: Urthona. Enitharmon, who is Urthona's feminine separated other, as Los is his masculine, weaves the "Bodies of Vegetation" for the divided spectres. The spectres are what mankind become when ruled by reason alone and when acceptance of contrary states of being has failed to take place.[45] In the final night of *The Four Zoas*, all four of the feminine counterparts take their place

---

[43] Gimbutas, op. cit., 196:

As a supreme Creator who creates from her own substance she is the primary goddess of the Old European pantheon. In this she contrasts with the Indo-European-Mother, who is the impalpable sacred earth-spirit, and is not in herself a creative principle; only through the interaction of the male sky-god does she become pregnant.

[44] Neumann, op. cit., 120.

[45] K.342, FZ. VIII:52:

Enitharmon wove in tears, singing songs of Lamentation
And pitying comfort as she sigh'd forth on the wind the Spectres,
Also the Vegetated bodies which Enitharmon wove
Open'd within their hearts & in their loins & in their brain

beside their looms.[46] Blake was aware of the key importance of opposites as, I suggest, was Homer. Not only are the *Iliad* and the *Odyssey* antithetical, but the stories contained within them are.

When Neumann discusses the primordial archetype he is also speaking of a contemporary archetype, albeit an unacknowledged one, which contains "positive and negative attributes."[47] This is an evolvement, for birth must have as its opposite, death; "the Feminine contains opposites, and the world actually lives because it combines earth and heaven, night and day, death and life."[48] Up to this point all is well. The acceptance of the opposition contained within the feminine archetype that precedes the division into good and bad goddess is as it should be. But the decline had started. By the time of Blake's writing, the acceptance of contraries was no longer occurring, and in fact the entire thrust of the poem *The Four Zoas* is about the necessity for acceptance of contraries, the recognition of a principial unity of masculine and feminine, spirit and soul, that transcends mere physical being.

★★★

Let us return to the reading of the *Iliad* as cautionary. We have read of the greed and pride shown by Agamemnon and the anger

---

To Beulah; & the Dead in Ulro descended from the War
Of Urizen & Tharmas & from the Shadowy female's clouds.
And some were woven [One fold *del.*] single, & some twofold, &
    some threefold
In Head or Heart or Reins, according to the fittest order
Of most merciful pity & compassion to the spectrous dead

[46] K.377–78, FZ.IX:778:

Then Enion & Ahania & Vala & the wife of dark Urthona
Rose from the feast, in joy ascending to their Golden Looms.
There the wing'd shuttle sang, the spindle & the distaff & the Reel
Rang sweet the praise of industry. Thro' all the golden rooms
Heaven rang with winged Exultation. All beneath howl'd loud;
With tenfold rout & desolation roar'd the Chasms beneath
Where the wide woof flow'd down & where the Nations are gather'd
together.

[47] Neumann, op. cit., 12.

[48] Ibid., 45.

of Achilles. And the exemplar of lust or love is shown in the cuck-older's scene with Helen and Paris. Now let us consider the two opposing gods of war. Athene, who up until this time appears to have been the goddess most revered by the city of Ilium and seen as its protector, has chosen to fight on the side of the Greeks and has turned her back on the Trojans. Again we must remember Kitto's theory concerning the imposition of a male god domi-nated culture. Athene, with her curious birth and her feminine attributes, makes her the ideal goddess to be absorbed into this culture. Ares is the god of war. I do not think that Ares' support of the Trojans is a default position. It is important for him to be the god of war, who is in support of the Trojans. Throughout the *Iliad* Ares' maniacal battle lust is continually mentioned; so it is logical that he be the war god who would support these syba-rites. It is, I think, important that this excess be seen as a "Trojan" attribute and that this be recognized and punished.

Appalled by the damage being wrought by the Trojans with the help of Ares, Hera and Athene set about to correct the situa-tion caused by "this madman Ares who regards not any law."[49] Presumably Hera and Athene are full of a sense of justice. Diomedes, with help from Athene, wounds Ares because he has disregarded his pledge not to engage in the battle on the side of the Trojans.[50] This is another example of untrustworthiness, as was Paris's escape from his duel. Both gods, who have shown this uncontrollable lust—be it for lovemaking or war—are injured appropriately. His father, Zeus, speaks of how he finds him the "most hateful" of the gods; "always strife is dear to you, and wars and fighting. You have the unbearable, overpowering spirit of your mother, Hera."[51] Zeus then speaks of how difficult it is to control Hera and reminds him that it is only his maternal parent-age that prevents him from being punished. So Ares retires from the fighting, retreating to the comfort of Olympus, where after berating him for his double dealing and his uncontrollable rage,

[49] *Il.* V:761.
[50] Ibid., 829–834.
[51] Ibid., 891–893.

Zeus also instructs the god of healing to care for him. Having successfully forced Ares to withdraw from the battle,

> then back to the halls of great Zeus went Argive Hera and
> Alalcomenean Athene, when they had made Ares, the bane
> of mortals, cease from his man-slaying.[52]

While it is true that the women in the *Iliad* are undervalued, underdrawn, undeveloped, the goddesses are shown as having more substance and are able to defeat "man-slaying" Ares. Hera and Athene are two very important goddesses seemingly controlled by Zeus but who nevertheless represent the female aspect of the divine.[53] That the feminine principle of the divine should be represented by these particular goddesses, and that they should be on the winning side, is fortuitous. As pre-Aryan and obviously well established, perhaps it was necessary to have them in this conflict on the side of the Greeks to strengthen the foundation myth of the Achaeans. Even Achilles, the greatest hero of them all who can defeat any male in combat, is compliant with the orders of Hera and Athene: "Goddess, one must observe the words of you two, no matter how angry he may be at heart, for it is better so."[54] Zeus, for all his strength and might, is outmanoeuvred and outflanked at times by Hera and Athene. Ilium was one of Zeus's favorite cities and yet he allows it to be destroyed. Zeus, the mighty sky god imposed upon a matriarchal order by the invasion of the Indo-Europeans, is persuaded, or appears to be persuaded, to do what he does not wish to do.

According to David Leeming and Jake Page, Hera, who began her life as part of the early matriarchal tradition, has become an ineffectual nag, married to an oversexed, despotic male in the

---

[52] Ibid., 907–909.

[53] Bonnie S. Anderson & Judith P. Zinsser, *A History of Their own*, 1989, Middlesex, Penguin Books, 16. Anderson and Zinsser incorrectly state that "Hera joins with Aphrodite in supporting the Greeks against the Trojans, and her vindictiveness leads to the total destruction of Troy." While correct in their assessment of Hera and what takes place in Troy, it is Athene who fights with her. Aphrodite supports the Trojans.

[54] *Il.I*:216.

Iliad.[55] The usurpation of matrilineal rights, the objectifying of women which Homer portrays to perfection, the idea taken up and used in modern warfare that ownership, if not rape, of women is itself a weapon of war—these are the conditions experienced by the females in the *Iliad.* One only has to remember Nestor's rousing the Greeks to fight with the following inducement:

> So let no man make haste to depart homewards until each
> has lain with the wife of some Trojan, and has got requital
> for his strivings and groanings over Helen.[56]

The blood, sweat, and tears are amply repaid if you manage to "lay" the wife of one of your opponents. Surely a small reward for a man but a large punishment for a woman who has done nothing but be. And just as surely, the women did not wish this to happen but were powerless to prevent it happening. Some would quibble that this is not rape, but they are usually of the masculine sex. Are we able to say that this same passivity is also portrayed by the female goddesses? Is Aryan Hera ineffectual in her role as helpless female unable to withstand her philandering husband? She is more than able to hold her own when she needs to do so. More to the point, has her support of the Achaeans further eroded the rights women previously held? The answer to this must be yes. But this is not because her methods are any different to those of Zeus, for seduction is often employed as the weapon of choice for either sex. Where this has allowed for a reduction in status for women is the masculine response to these actions. She is shown as crafty and untrustworthy because she

---

[55] David Leeming & Jake Page, *Goddess, Myths of the Female Divine,* 1994, New York, Oxford University Press, 133:

> Hera, who in her pre-Aryan form had been an incarnation of Goddess as Earth and Mother in Anatolia, Crete, and Samos, became in Olympian Greece the unsympathetic, shrewish wife of the philandering Achaean thunder god, Zeus. As the goddess of marriage, she appeared to lend female approbation to the very institution by which the old matrilineal rights were most clearly usurped by the patriarchy that saw wives as belonging, like other valuable objects, to their husbands. In short, her ancient fertility function was sublimated in values antithetical to her essence

[56] *Il. II*:354–356.

employs this method. This is a value judgement employed by predominantly male critics and translators. One may certainly question her methods but that questioning must also extend to the methods employed by Zeus.

When Hera sees Poseidon rallying the Achaeans while Zeus is having a rest on Mount Ida, it is an opportunity too good to miss: "Then she took thought, the ox-eyed queenly Hera, how she might distract the mind of Zeus who bears the aegis."[57] Hera promises one of the Graces to Sleep if he puts Zeus to sleep after they have made love, a love-making enhanced by Aphrodite's powers fraudulently obtained by Hera. While Zeus is asleep in Hera's arms, Poseidon is to fire up the Argives. He does this so well that Hector has to be withdrawn from the battle. These are the practical results desired by Hera.

Her story, to Aphrodite and Zeus, is that Tethys and Oceanus are having difficulties in their marriage and that she will act as peacemaker for them.[58] Hera's province is traditionally concerned with marriage and the lives of women; therefore her fabrication is so convincing that neither listener shows doubt. She bathes, anoints herself, borrows Aphrodite's inlaid strap "in which are fashioned all manner of allurements,"[59] and sets out to seduce Zeus. Their joining together in love is as close a description to *hieros gamos* as we see in the *Iliad*:

> At that the son of Cronos clasped his wife in his arms, and beneath them the bright earth made fresh-sprung grass to grow, and dewy lotus, and crocus, and hyacinth thick and soft that kept them from the ground. On this they lay, and were clothed about with a cloud, fair and golden, from which fell drops of glistening dew.[60]

With their union the world springs into fruition. One could say that Aphrodite's inlaid strap is used by both husband and wife. By

---

[57] *Il. XIV*:159–160.

[58] Ibid., 205–207: "loose for them their endless strife, for now for a long time they have been holding aloof from one another, from the marriage bed and from love, since wrath has fallen on their hearts."

[59] Ibid., 214–215.

[60] Ibid., 346–349.

promising Pasithea, one of the Graces, and using the bait of love, Hera uses Sleep to quieten Zeus. Sleep has "been longing . . . all my days," to win Pasithea.[61] After the love-making between Zeus and Hera, he is lulled to sleep and Poseidon will ensure that the Argives fight.

One wonders, if Zeus is so powerful and all knowing, why did he not know that this would occur? When Zeus wakes and sees the havoc being wrought by the Achaeans, his immediate and correct reaction is to blame Hera. The threatened punishment is enough to cause Hera to protest her innocence and blame Poseidon. Is it pretence on Zeus's part that he believes her? He instructs Hera on her next moves and outlines the pattern of the war that will now take place. Poseidon is forced to back down although he states that he is equal to Zeus, who is first-born. Hera is obedient to Zeus. So Hera, a pre-Aryan Mother Goddess, a goddess of the city, has used feminine wiles to get her way and then lied about her involvement. This deceitful behavior is portrayed as a particularly unpleasant, female attribute, even though we have seen this in the behavior of the masculine gods or mortals, and it is used to reduce Hera's standing, not in the eyes of the other gods, but in the wider audience. Her behavior is then extrapolated across the wider society, making women seem, in general, untrustworthy, conniving creatures. Now it is difficult for a woman to stand toe to toe with a man in order to get her way. She has certain tools she is able to use to obtain her ends. Maybe we should call her wise or shrewd to choose such tools as will bring her the result she desires. When Zeus, or a lesser, mortal male, evades telling the truth, they are praised for their cunning. So, logically, we should praise Hera for hers. Or is Homer just presenting us with the folly of human behavior writ large when enacted by the gods, whether male or female?

Athene, the goddess of war and wisdom, is supportive of Hera and does the bidding of both Zeus and Hera. Gimbutas traces the origin of Athene back to the Snake and Bird Goddesses of Old Europe. In this role Athene is the symbol of re-creation, the very essence of the feminine principle, and yet Gimbutas asks how did

---

[61] *Il. XIV*:159–160.

"Athena become a goddess of war?" Gimbutas says that Athena was in a direct line from Minoan culture and a protectress of the city.[62] I think the more important point is that Athene, when she is taken up into the Olympic pantheon, is a virgin. No longer can she be seen in a maternal light, so that her role as protectress of the city is only that of a war god. Prefiguring her role in the *Odyssey*, Homer does however acknowledge Athene's maternal aspect. Odysseus defeats Ajax in a foot race at the funeral games. Ajax says:

> Well now! The goddess hampered me in my running, she who stands ever by Odysseus' side like a mother, and helps him.[63]

Nevertheless she is only one god of war in the Homeric tradition. What is interesting is that the other war god, Ares, is depicted as being uncontrollable in contrast to Athene. This is a characteristic more often attributed to the female than the male, and as stated earlier, this uncontrollable blood lust shown by Ares suits as a means of demonizing the enemy, the Trojans.[64]

Gimbutas sees Aphrodite in the role of a mother goddess:

> Aphrodite Urania, born from the sea, was portrayed as flying through the air standing or sitting on a goose or being accompanied by three geese in the Greek terracottas of the sixth and fifth centuries BC; like Athena, she maintains certain Old European features of the Bird Goddess. Homer regarded Cyprus as her true home, but pre-Phoenician Cyprus was within the sphere of Minoan culture. There is strong reason to believe that "Aphrodite" was a goddess-name originally common to the language of both islands. It is also believed that the Cretan name "Ariadne," "the very

---

[62] Gimbutas, op. cit., 149.

[63] *Il. XXIII*: 782–783.

[64] Ares has a female companion in battle called Enyo. In Michael Grant & John Hazel's *Who's Who in Classical Mythology*, 2002, Abingdon, Routledge, 121, she is described as "A goddess of battle, the companion of Ares." Her appearance in the *Iliad* is brief, V:333, where her epithet is "sacker of cities" and V:593, as "queen Enyo." She was taken up in Roman mythology as Bellona and became an important cult figure.

Holy One," was an early Hellenic description for Aphrodite herself (Farnell 1927:18).[65]

Aphrodite, another example of the fertile Earth Goddess in the Old European tradition, becomes a wimpish inciter of lust and sexual passion. Does this devalue cohabitation, lust, or Aphrodite? If it is Aphrodite who is devalued, she becomes more so in Book V, when Diomedes charges, "knowing that she was a weakling goddess,"[66] and wounds her. She is wounded in the wrist just below the Mound of Venus at the base of the thumb through an imperishable robe, a wound that causes ichor to flow. The very clear sexual symbolism emphasizes the disconnection between Sex and War. It is important, however, to remember why Aphrodite is on the battlefield. It is in defence of her son, Aeneas, that she is present as he battles against Diomedes, who is assisted by Athene.

> About her dear son she flung her white arms, and in front of him she spread a fold of her bright garment to be a shelter against missiles, lest any of the Danaans with swift horses might hurl a spear of bronze into his chest and take away his life.[67]

The wound causes Aphrodite to withdraw from a conflict that she has caused. Diomedes has been instructed and empowered by Athene to strike Aphrodite as she seeks to protect her son. Athene and Hera mock Aphrodite for her limp-wristedness but Zeus speaks kindly to her: "Not to you, my child, are given works of war; but attend to the lovely works of marriage."[68] Here Zeus acknowledges Aphrodite's role in producing the loveliness of marriage, thus giving that state an importance we have not yet seen in the *Iliad* except in passing with Hector and Andromache, and yet she is also on the losing side. In Blake's work *The Four Zoas*, Luvah (Love) and his feminine emanation Vala (Nature), are instructed to return to their own place, "the place of seed" in

[65] Gimbutas, op. cit., 149.
[66] *Il.*V: 331.
[67] Ibid., 314–317.
[68] Ibid., 428–429.

much the same manner; that is, marriage, the union of opposites, only functions correctly if it is guided by Love in its right place. In her actions towards Aeneas, Aphrodite has fulfilled the protective role of mother to perfection. Protecting her son, she, an immortal, is wounded. Of the two mothers, Hera and Aphrodite, only she displays this protective behavior towards her offspring.

Thetis, a lesser goddess, is another mother and also quick to act in defence of her child, doing whatever is necessary to advance the cause of her offspring, Achilles. She acts as intermediary for Achilles with Zeus, and her request on behalf of her son places Almighty Zeus in an invidious position. His answer to Thetis is that it will cause him strife with the wife.[69] By agreeing to Thetis's request to assist Achilles, Zeus rouses Hera's suspicions. Although he has been surreptitious with this agreement, Hera is able, through divine omniscience, intuition, past experience or sheer bloody-mindedness, to identify the goddess and her request. Hera is presented with an established position by Zeus; that is, he may well wish for a quiet life without Hera's suspicions and arguments, but when he makes a decision she and everyone else must accept it. Persuaded by Hephaestus, the son whom she herself damaged, Hera withdraws from confrontation and, after the banquet, lies beside Zeus. Does this retreat make Hera passive, manipulative, or a shrewd general who marshals her forces for use at the appropriate time?

At the end of the truce which had been negotiated in order that Menelaus and Paris fight for Helen, Zeus taunts Hera and Athene about their support for the Argives, and Aphrodite for her love of Paris. As a result of Aphrodite's intervention, Zeus allocates victory to Menelaus and raises the possibility of a peace pact between the armies, with Helen being awarded to Menelaus. This infuriates both Athene and Hera, as they have done much to expedite victory for Agamemnon's troops, and they are distraught that all their finagling will have been for nought. Serious negotiations now commence between Zeus and Hera as they fight and argue the rights of either side. Zeus relinquishes his rights to Ilium with the proviso that Hera must do the same

---

[69] *Il.*I:518–521.

thing, without argument, when he wishes to raze a city that she loves. Hera agrees to this, offering him Argos, Sparta, and Mycenae, and as we are not told whether Hera was ever called upon to honor her promise, in effect what we have here is a victory for the Goddess. Or, do we? Two of these cities were home to a mother goddess while the other has women occupying a far more equal place in that society. Is this another success on the part of Zeus? By ceding them to him if and when he requests them, is not Hera allowing for the takeover of the Olympian Gods? Perhaps it is not only the rout of Troy that occurs in the *Iliad*—a success story for the warlike Achaeans—but also the whittling away of the position of the earlier gods, as Leeming and Page have said.

Agamemnon is convinced that the breaking of the truce means Zeus will be on the side of the non truce-breakers. Of course he is right, but Zeus is also the cause of the truce-breaking. Once again the uroboric nature of the behavior between man and god is apparent. Who is causing what? Athene supports the Argives while Ares, God of War, with Terror, Rout, and his sister Strife, support the Trojans when battle is commenced. When Ares is wounded and withdraws, Hera and Athene—both of whom are polis goddesses if not mother goddesses—have defeated the God of War. They have done this not by choosing feminine weapons, whatever they may be, but by out-muscling the most aggressive male god. Therefore they have set the mode of behavior for the female goddesses in the Olympian pantheon. Although as guardians of a city, polis goddesses, they would have been required to protect that city, nevertheless they appear to be more war-like than the god of War.

Zeus decides to honor his promise made to Thetis. His decree is issued and all must obey it.[70] Athene is not quiescent and asks for the right to be a tactician only, and Zeus's reply is enigmatic. Hera and Athene, unlike their masculine counterparts, are unable to accept Zeus's decree. They attempt to join the battle but are intercepted by Iris on Zeus's instructions. She repeats his orders, with some embellishments, and they comply. Interest-

[70] *Il.VIII*:5–9.

ingly, Zeus expects this rebellion from Hera—which brings into question Leeming and Page's description of her as just a nag—but wants to teach his daughter a lesson. In Book XI, the Achaeans fight back, aided and abetted by Athene and Hera to such an extent that Zeus has to rescue Hector. Zeus's plan is to allow Hector to reach the ships for two reasons: to honor his promise to Thetis and to enhance Hector's reputation, after death, in so doing. These will be Hector's final moments of glory, for Achilles' treatment of his body after death will be inglorious. Such is the vigor of the assault that even the withdrawn Achilles notices something is happening. By now the ramparts are being stormed, although the final destruction of these walls belongs to Poseidon and Apollo. It will be their right to demolish this construction by men. With the assistance of Zeus, Hector is invincible. So much so that he is unable to listen to the voice of cool reason, Polydamas, who argues against an assault of the ships after the sign given by the eagle and serpent. The battle for the wall rages on and on. Page after page follow concerning stories of bravery and valor. Men, trailing glory, descend to the afterlife; Epicles, Glaucus, Alcmaon, all joined together in the neutrality of death. Hector, with the aid of Zeus, manages to hurl a stone through the gates: "None that met him could have held him back, none save the gods, when once he leapt inside the gates; and his eyes blazed with fire."[71] Having ensured that his promise to Thetis is well on its way to fulfilment, at this point Zeus withdraws from the battle.

The uncontrollable anger displayed by Achilles now reaps what is, for him, its most serious result. Patroclus, weeping for his wounded comrades, berates Achilles for his anger and asks that he may lead the Myrmidons into battle: "So he spoke in prayer, great fool that he was, for it was certain to be his own evil death and fate for which he prayed."[72] Achilles allows him to do this providing he does not diminish Achilles' glory by fighting the Trojans to the walls. Patroclus, of course, is unable to fulfil that requirement, as the rush of glory is too much. It is he who is the agent for

---

[71] *Il. XII*:465–466.
[72] *Il. XVI*:46–47.

Sarpedon's death. Zeus wavers at the choice of death and life for his child, much to Hera's disapproval. Her words reinforce the differences between gods and mortals and stiffen Zeus's backbone, which is a reversal of their relative positions. A mother goddess ensuring that death will occur when it is fated, while the father is undecided as to the right decision: "Most dread son of Cronos, what a word have you said! Are you minded to free from dolorous death a mortal man, one doomed long since by fate?'[73] When Hector faces death at the walls, Zeus is again undecided. Athene, using the same words, reminds him that Hector must die.[74] All that Zeus is able to do for his son is ensure that his corpse will be transported to his own land, where he will be properly mourned. Patroclus, on the other hand, has suffered from what many mortals suffer, that is, he has become enamoured of his own ability and has attempted to take the walls of Troy. He was unable to do this for very good reasons, not the least of which was that Zeus had not decreed that he should. With the assistance of Apollo and Euphorbus, Hector defeats and kills Patroclus.

Menelaus, whose singular ineptitude has led to this debacle, now plays a pivotal role in ending it as, with help, the corpse of Patroclus is retrieved. We are not given many insights into the contestants, and in particular into Menelaus. Homer now shows us how Menelaus sees the events that preceded the onslaught against Troy—that is, the seduction and removal of his wife by a guest. The picture we gain is that of a trusting, hospitable, country-type chap. One who might assume that a guest would not do the wrong thing? Maybe this is a family characteristic. Certainly Agamemnon, Menelaus's brother, shares his lack of suspicion regarding his own wife. Or maybe this is a masculine underestimation of their feminine partners.

Thetis realizes that the moment of her son's death is nigh. Her lament is any mother's lament and has little to do with her goddess status. She goes to Achilles, who bemoans the fact that he has caused his comrade's death and that he is unable to fight, for his armor is now being worn by Hector. Thetis leaves to obtain

[73] Ibid., 440–442.
[74] *Il. XXII*: 179–180.

immortal armor from Hephaestus, leaving Achilles with strict instructions that he will have to wait until tomorrow to fight, and like a good son he obeys his mother. Meanwhile, Hera, via Iris, is instructing Achilles to do something about saving the body of Patroclus. Obeying his mother, Achilles also obeys Hera. When Thetis arrives at Hephaestus's dwelling we meet Charis, wife of Hephaestus, fleetingly. A gentle, hospitable woman, who welcomes Thetis into their home. Charis summons Hephaestus and directs him to help Thetis. Although this is our only glimpse of Charis and her role appears to be a domestic one, she is also shown as having equality with Hephaestus, by her instruction to him that Thetis needs help and that he heed her.

Enhanced by Athene, Achilles gives a battle cry three times, which cry creates a pause in the proceedings thus enabling the Argives to drag Patroclus's body clear. Interestingly it is Hera who now calls a halt to the fighting. Does this mean that woman is always able to control the masculine urge to dominate and fight?

> Then was the unwearying Sun sent by ox-eyed queenly Hera
> to return, unwilling, to the stream of Ocean. So the sun set
> and the noble Achaeans ceased from the mighty strife and
> the evil war.[75]

It is true that Zeus has set the limits on how far and how long the fighting will last by declaring this is in Book XVII: "for still I shall grant glory to the Trojans, to slay and slay, until they come to the well-benched ships, and the sun sets and holy darkness comes on"[76]—but it is Hera who decides that the day will end when she drives the reluctant sun to its bed.

Zeus questions Hera regarding her relationship with the Achaeans. The contrast between Hera and Thetis as mothers is demonstrated further by Thetis's relationship with Hephaestus. Thetis, in effect, mothered the crippled god when Hera threw him out. Their motherly attitudes are very different. Thetis orders her son, Achilles, to do one thing in Book XVIII, while

[75] *Il. XVIII*:240–242.
[76] *Il. XVII*:453–454.

Hera commands another action. Thetis's orders are given to protect her son, that is, that he must not fight until he is wearing armor. Hera on the other hand is eager to gain an offensive against the Trojans and has a far more cavalier attitude towards the rights of mortals than Thetis. Thetis is the good mother while Hera is the bad, caring for neither Hephaestus nor Achilles; it is a very clear difference given to us by Homer.

It is Thetis's fate to bear a mortal child subject to death, a death that will happen very soon, but she continues to do whatever she can to help her son. Hera is far more sanguine concerning her children. They are on their own and even Zeus displays more mothering instinct than she does. Zeus wavers in his desire to be fair to Thetis in Book XXII, but Athene does not when the scales fall. Athene, disguised as Deiphobus, Hector's brother, urges him to stand and fight, "by such words and by guile did Athene lead him on."[77] Achilles kills Hector and, shaming his death, drags him back to the ships through the dust. When news of Hector's death reaches Troy, Hector's wife Andromache weeps for her lost husband and vows to destroy the work of women's hands, that is, woven objects.

★★★

What knowledge of the female gods do we now possess? There is a fine mingling in their attributes. Aphrodite is a loving, laughing goddess who attempts to be what she is not in her confrontation with Diomedes. She does so in defence of her son. Her moment of anger with Helen is more an aberration than a characteristic. She is feminine and weak, yet her attributes are used by Hera when she needs to subdue Zeus, the greatest of the gods. Athene, the goddess of war and wisdom, is supportive of Hera and does the bidding of both Zeus and Hera when it suits her ends. Hera displays a motherlike affection for the Achaeans but fails to show this anywhere else.

Throughout the *Iliad* Homer makes reference to the lion as a symbol of strength, courage, and fighting ability. There are wonderful descriptive passages about the lion's tawny mane, his ability to fight and win, all associated with moments in the battle. In

---

[77] *Il. XXII*:247.

truth, it is the lioness that does most of the protecting, stalking of prey, fighting, killing, feeding, in order to nurture the pride. The lion's ability is mostly reserved for roaring and begetting, a perfect simile for Zeus. Athene then is a prime example of the female of the species protecting her young by her ability to fight, her young in this case the Achaeans. A female's ability to fight may well be restricted by her attributes, as in the case of Aphrodite. But Athene is not so circumscribed. Born, as she is, from the head of Zeus, she nevertheless retains her links with Old European mythology through her attribute of wisdom and her skill in weaving. Athene's virginity, so designated by the Greeks, appears to alienate her from any aspect of "mother goddess." If Gimbutas is correct, then she is a product of Indo-European and Oriental beliefs. That descent from the line of "mother goddesses" is effectively finished when Athene is upheld as a permanent virgin. While it is difficult to think of any god who is a virgin, at this time, and it is only the goddesses who are designated as virgin, the desire for the pure female does not appear to extend to mortals. Briseis, untouched by Agamemnon but not by Achilles, is still able to talk of marriage with her despoiler.

Hera is most definitely not a virgin goddess. Leeming and Page describe her as an "unsympathetic, shrewish wife," and that is a value judgement in itself. To whom was she unsympathetic? Her husband, as he fertilized anything that didn't move? Her children, all of whom had the same strengths as she? Is Hera merely a wife dominated by a husband who is the supreme ruler? If that is so, then Hera manages to get her own way on all manner of issues. It is her desire that the Trojans be defeated and that Troy fall. The detour, which is the story of the *Iliad*, is arrived at because Zeus promises Thetis that her son shall be repaid for the insult given him by Agamemnon. Zeus's obligation and promise to Thetis is something he feels he must conceal from Hera. When Zeus's promise is fulfilled—that is, when the fighting has reached the ships—it is Hera who calls a halt to the day and the fighting. Hera's attitude towards the Argives appears so maternal and protective that it calls from Zeus the accusation that they had sprung from her loins:

You have then had your way, ox-eyed queenly Hera; you have roused Achilles, swift of foot. The long-haired Achaeans must surely be children of your own womb.[78]

Phillip Slater sees Hera's role as mother of Hephaestus as emasculating and threatening.[79] But what is important about Hera in the *Iliad* is that she is mother to the Achaeans, "children from her own womb," not that she is a mother to an individual god who possesses the same strengths as her. Both Hera and Athene are rewritten from polis to Olympian goddesses in this epic.

It is true that Zeus commands and expects total obedience to his commands. He speaks of Hera as a nagging wife, but is quite easily seduced by her when she feels it necessary. Hera is like a child's weighted doll which, when knocked, hits the ground and bounces back up again. She is ordered about, threatened, and, indeed, punished, but it is impossible for her to accept a position that does not have her wholehearted approval. Zeus is like the lion: he has the roar, while the lioness, Hera, has the grunt. Her reply to the dread son of Cronos is of interest.

> Even a human being, I suppose, is likely to accomplish what he wills for another man, one who is only mortal and knows not all the wisdom that is mine. How then was I, who say that I am the best of goddesses—doubly so, since I am eldest and am called your wife, and you are king among all the immortals—how was I not in my resentment against the Trojans to stitch evils for them?[80]

If even a human being is able to see something to its desired end then why not the "best of goddesses"?

★★★

What has been presented in the *Iliad* may well be a reduction in the role of the female from the pre-historical position, with some exceptions in the roles of the goddesses. The question must be asked, is Homer creating this iconography of male and female duality or is he demonstrating the loss of that principial unity?

---

[78] *Il. XVIII*:357–359.

[79] Phillip Slater, *The Glory of Hera: Greek Mythology and the Greek Family*, 1992, Princeton, Princeton University Press, 194.

[80] *Il. XVIII*:362–367.

One would have to say that the loss of principial unity is clearly shown in this poem. The Trojans, who demonstrated some appreciation of the female virtues—house, home, children, honoring the goddess Athene—have been demolished by the invading Aryans. The female goddesses are taken up into the Olympic pantheon but their roles are changed. In much the same manner as any female who takes on roles that were previously masculine and using more masculine techniques, the feminine virtues are lost in the battle to be supreme. Of the three main goddesses, Aphrodite is the only one to display maternal love, thus remaining true to her earlier incarnation. Of the mothers, mortal and immortal, three are on the losing side and one will lose her semi-immortal son. Zeus's acknowledgement of "the loveliness of marriage" and support for Aphrodite's role does not translate into practical support for this ideal in the mortal or immortal world. Uncontrollable emotions displayed by mortal or immortal are all punished in some way, and this includes the revolt of the lower classes represented by Thersites' outburst.[81] But this cautionary tale teaches lessons that are not always obvious. If the big three goddesses, Hera, Athene, and Aphrodite, were directly linked to the mother goddesses of pre-history, their roles are altered by inclusion in the Olympic pantheon. They are powerful goddesses in this pantheon, but with the exception of Aphrodite, mother-love is not displayed by them in the *Iliad*. Homer does however present us with a different view of Athene in the *Odyssey*. That the role of the mother is acknowledged to some extent by the Trojans is to no avail. Knox, quoting Simone Weil, makes the point that we are lovers of violence and that this is the appeal of the *Iliad*. Weil says of the *Iliad* that it is a poem about force:

> The true hero, the true subject, the center of the *Iliad*, is force. . . . Those who had dreamed that force, thanks to progress, now belonged to the past, have seen the poem as a historic document; those who can see that force, today as in the past, is at the center of all human history, find in the *Iliad* is most beautiful, its purest mirror.[82]

---

[81] *Il. II*:260.

[82] Knox, *Iliad*, Introduction and Notes, op. cit., quoting Simone Weil, 29.

But Homer also has a subtext. More than anything else I think that the poem is about excess of passion and how that is punished. Therefore this poem is about moderation. Pity, as an emotion, is exhibited sparingly. The gods, especially the male gods, feel pity, but it is not the transcendent pity of Los and Enitharmon.[83] The role of women is tenuous and sad; the role of the goddesses may well have altered from their original conception. Marriage, as an institution, has become, as Rose says, a means of controlling inheritance, a situation that does not change in some levels of society. In saying this one must also remember where *hieros gamos,* sacred marriage, is shown. It is there in the seduction of Zeus by Hera; there in the sweetness and firmness of Charis; and most definitely there in the creation of the shield by Hephaestus. These beautiful lines by Homer show the world in all its gore and glory. When he has made the earth, heavens, sea, sun, moon, and stars, then he makes

> two fair cities of mortal men. In the one there were marriages and feastings, and by the light of the blazing torches they were leading the brides from their rooms through the city, and loud rose the bridal song.[84]

This is the first city described, but the other is very different: "But around the other city lay two armies of warriors gleaming in armor."[85] The only song heard in this city is the cry of battle. There are two ways to interpret the shield. One is to say that marriage is so important that Homer places it first in the description. This may be so, but it is not what we have seen in the *Iliad.* The other is to say that there is balance in this description—each city occupies half the shield—but we have not seen that either. Complementarity and balance are aims which he saw as important. The idea that male and female complement each other is lost in the *Iliad,* but sexual complementarity is restored by Homer in the *Odyssey.*

[83] I have mentioned Zeus's desire to spare Sarpedon, but in Book XXIV, Zeus, Apollo, the gods, and Achilles are shown as exhibiting pity towards the Trojans. See lines 18–19, 23, 174, 357, for examples.

[84] *Il. IVIII*: 490–503.

[85] Ibid., 509–510.

Useful though it is, Kitto's historical account of the Homeric theology is not nearly enough. Kitto is writing a history of religious development in the Achaean-occupied north-eastern Mediterranean basin. Homer, according to Herodotus, is creating a religion. What was worshipped in Homer's account of the marriage between Zeus and Hera, mistress of the marriage? It is not, at first, easy to see. At the same time, for any devotee of their divinities, the shocking state of the marriage does not lead to an historical analysis but to a profound sense that the reader's own marriage could be a good deal worse than it is. Homer's vision is an astonishing union of constancy in chaos as the sexes battle it out in a traditional marriage. The moral example is powerful. But the moral level of symbolic analysis is only one of Dante's four levels and not the most noble or divine.

This moral example also covers the behavior of Agamemnon and Achilles. Both display pride and anger as if these emotions were a badge of honor. Both die ignominious deaths, Agamemnon at the hand of his wife, a warrior beaten by a woman; Achilles by an arrow shot by a lowly bowman. Striving for glory, their deaths are ordinary and banal. It seems that the basis of the Apollonian doctrine of moderation is here in the *Iliad*. While I agree with Kitto that ἀρετή, or excellence, is an important part of the human striving in this poem, I also think the idea that a tall poppy be cut down is also at the base of their thought. We must not forget the importance of Moira, Fate. Hera reminds Zeus of this when he hesitates about the death of his beloved son, Sarpedon. Moira, a female goddess, controls even the strongest of Gods. I think that the importance of Fate to the Greeks was not that they may change their ends, but that their ends were suited to the life they had lived. When we consider the deaths of Agamemnon and Achilles, it seems that there is a retributive element to these. If they had acted in a more reasoned manner, would their deaths have been more in keeping with their positions? The reading that the "sins of the father" contributed to Agamemnon's death is often proposed, but if that was the cause, how did Menelaus escape? Unless we consider that living with Helen was a punishment. And what had Achilles' father done to call down such a death on his son? The blame must belong to the individual. Each of these men earned their fates. Even the gods compromise when it is necessary. Hera must sacrifice two of her most favored cities to win victory for the Greeks. Achilles knew that he had two fates to choose from, as all do. His choice was between a long and peaceful life, or one that is short and glorious. He wanted to be remembered as a hero, and for some he achieved that goal. But I doubt he would have desired the death he was given, as there was little glory in that. So it appears that knowledge of what your fate may be does not encompass all that you would choose. Again, this is true for all. "Man proposes, God disposes" appears to be as true for the Greeks as it is for us. And we must not forget that Homer showed these choices very clearly in the Shield of Achilles.

Certain qualities in the human appear to be required by the goddesses and gods. Not acknowledging their presence and their assistance is calamitous. When compared to them, man is puny, even Achilles. They are such an integral part of the life of these people that you wonder how Agamemnon could slight the priest of Apollo and think it was right to do so. But introspection was never an attribute of the Atridae. Being aware that as mortals, if you are successful it is with their help, but if you fail you have in some way offended them and you must learn how that has occurred. In the next chapter we will see how this changes the life of Odysseus.

6

The Goddess, Woman
and Marriage in the *Odyssey*

LET US TURN to the *Odyssey* and its central character Odysseus, and compare this poem with the *Iliad*, although in so doing I am reminded of Eliade's statement concerning our understanding of myth:

> the mythology of Homer and Hesiod continued to interest the elites in all parts of the Hellenistic world. But the myths were no longer taken literally: what was now sought was their "hidden meanings" (*hyponoiai*: the term "*allegoria*" was used later).[1]

Of course, by virtue of race, status, religion, and, in the case of this author, gender, we are so far removed from Homeric thinking that there is little else that can be done but interpret allegorically. What must strike any reader of both epics is that there are major differences, if not in language then in content, and that this is so must be for a very good reason. The *Iliad* apparently champions the notion of excellence, and in particular excellence in fighting and dying; in the *Odyssey* this is replaced by something Taylor described as, "a voyage over the stormy sea of generation," that is, a life. My argument is that the *Iliad* is a poem that describes the end result of excess and warns against this, and I propose that the *Odyssey* is similar to that other Apollonian dictum: "know thyself."

In the opening verses of the *Odyssey* we meet a very different Odysseus. The shrewd tactician, the able debater, the brave

---

[1] Mircea Eliade, *Myth and Reality*, 1964, London, Allen Unwin, 154.

fighter, the man who demonstrates ably the ἀρετή of these characteristics, is observed by Athene and Zeus from Olympus as he is held in thrall by Calypso: "But Odysseus, in his longing to see were it but the smoke leaping up from his own land, yearns to die."[2] We remember the heroic stand he makes in Book XI of the *Iliad* when he is alone on the battlefield. There Odysseus has cause to believe that his death may be imminent, but his proud heart does not let this deter him. He is a soldier and will fight even if alone, "So then around Odysseus, dear to Zeus, did the Trojans press."[3] This is the man we have known. A man conscious of the odds against him but prepared to face them. A man very different to Menelaus who, when he is in the same situation, chooses to seek help rather than die, while Odysseus adheres to the heroic tradition, where it is better to die bravely than to whimper for help.[4] We can say of course that Homer could not have Menelaus die when the purpose of this war is for him to regain possession of his wife. But the contrast between Odysseus and Menelaus seems deliberate. This may give more validity to Rose's theory that Menelaus represents an aspiring plutocracy, although I find it doubtful that Menelaus was in any way aspirational. Sequentially, the *Iliad* is followed by the *Odyssey*, and it is less easy to fit this poem into the plutocratic model. Perhaps Plato's view of Menelaus is closer to the truth. Socrates is speaking to a proverb, which he has rewritten to suit his purposes:

> *To the feasts of the good the good unbidden go;*
> and this alteration may be supported by the authority of Homer himself, who not only demolishes but literally outrages the proverb. For, after picturing Agamemnon as the most valiant of men, he makes Menelaus, who is but a faint-hearted warrior, come unbidden to the banquet of Agamemnon, who is feasting and offering sacrifices, not the better to the worse, but the worse to the better.[5]

[2] *Od.I*:57–59.

[3] *Il.XI*:419–420.

[4] *Il.XVII*:91–105.

[5] Plato, *Symposium*, trans. Jowett, 1952, Chicago, Encyclopaedia Britannica, 150.

I think that just as Homer wants us to consider the fundamental differences between Menelaus and Odysseus on the battlefield in the *Iliad,* so we are to consider the differences within their marriages in the *Odyssey.* The contrast between the carefully posed marriage of Menelaus and Helen and the disarray that is Odysseus's is striking. Menelaus regains his beautiful wife, who apparently keeps him tranquilized with more than enough wealth and a comfortable life after death as a son-in-law to Zeus—although one does wonder if this boon is extended to all Helen's husbands. One may well ask, "what more could life offer?" In order to regain his wife, Menelaus has called upon the might of the Achaeans, and they have responded gloriously. The Iliadic Odysseus is secure in the honor system he lives under, and his wife and child do not interfere with those beliefs. It is not of them he thinks when he stands alone against the Trojans, but of dying with glory. How then has this strong man become the man he is when first we meet him in the *Odyssey*? Odysseus stands on the shore all day, longing for his home and wife, and turning his back on all the pleasures living with a goddess has to offer. Or the man we see as suppliant to Queen Arete, who goes on his knees before her? "Arete, daughter of godlike Rhexenor, to your husband and to your knees have I come suppliant after many toils."[6] He neither dissembles with Queen Arete nor tries to present a kinder picture of himself when he tells her of his time on Ogygia, Calypso's island: "There for seven years I remained continually, and always with my tears I kept wet the immortal clothes which Calypso gave me."[7] Nor does he resemble the great speaker, sent by his king, to reason with Achilles. This man wants to turn his back on immortality, on agelessness, on a very easy life with a good-looking goddess who fancies him. And his reason for denying her the pleasure of his company is his longing for home, where his life will be mortal, he will grow old, and he will do as all must do in this generated world, which is struggle for the union of soul and spirit and then die.

6 *Od. VII*: 146–147.
7 Ibid., 259–260.

The *Odyssey* is written in the manner in which we view our life; it starts at the point where he is, remembers the past and imagines the future. E.H. Carr says historians must "view the past and achieve our understanding of the past, only through the eyes of the present."[8] Only in this way may a historian understand the past and anticipate the future. Only in this way may Odysseus regain his wife and kingdom. Achilles' story is like the flight of an arrow, whereas Odysseus's is muddled, tortuous, in the manner of an ordinary human life. Few, male or female, can measure themselves against Achilles and not be dwarfed by that almighty anger. Odysseus on the other hand is someone with whom it is possible to sympathize, to grieve, to be joyous—one to measure against and compare oneself with. He, Odysseus, is someone who possesses characteristics that we either admire or dislike in ourselves; in short, someone with whom we are able to identify. Odysseus is us—ordinary human beings attempting to live our lives and achieve the goals we set ourselves. The *Odyssey* is everyman's search for spiritual awareness as he travels the "stormy sea" of life.

The *Iliad* is teleological. It is the story of Achilles' wrath and the sequential happenings that occur because of that wrath. The *Odyssey,* like the *Iliad,* is another story concerning a male, "the male"—masculinity versus femininity. But what a difference! Johnson, as previously quoted, has said that there is a lack of feminine heroes in Western mythic literature and that Western love stories have tragic or fatal endings. The *Odyssey* is a love story with an extremely successful ending, using Johnson's terms, and is a part of the foundation of Western mythic literature. Johnson's criticisms are inaccurate. Odysseus does not turn his back on feminine attributes, and in fact wholeheartedly embraces them, as he does many of the females he meets. It is as if his cohabitation with a female goddess allows him to absorb the qualities owned by that goddess. As Blake says: "The desire of Man being Infinite, the possession is Infinite & himself Infinite."[9] Odysseus' dalliances with the immortal goddesses may have

[8] E.H Carr, *What is History?*, 1985, London, Penguin Books, 24.
[9] *K.97, TNN:VII.*

been an attempt to educate or enlighten himself, to allow insight into a world beyond mortals. The desire to know the infinite as far as any mortal is able appears to be the driving force behind Odysseus's often reluctant journey. At every important turning point in the story, Odysseus is assisted or hampered by a female, either mortal or immortal. Odysseus's wife's recognition is based upon the most fundamental part of the marriage, the marriage bed itself. Odysseus's description of the bed formed by him, with its Tree of Life significance, is the guarantee of Penelope's recognition of her other half, her husband.

> But do not now be angry with me for this, nor full of indignation, because at first, when I saw you, I did not give you welcome as I do now. . . . But now, since you have already recounted the tokens of our bed plain for all to see, which no other mortal has ever seen except you and me alone and one single handmaid, the daughter of Actor, whom my father gave me before I ever came here, her who kept the doors of our strong bridal chamber—now you convince my heart, for all its stubbornness.[10]

At this acknowledgment by his wife, Odysseus, the wily tactician and brave fighter, "wept, holding in his arms his beloved truehearted wife."[11] This is the man who is able to clear the halls of his enemies, a brave son, a father willing to allow his son to stand beside him, and a loving husband able to weep for love without shame. A man able to acknowledge that he feels emotional pain that is, given our previous encounter with him, an extraordinary about-turn.

★★★

Let us look briefly at the references to Demeter, the Mother Goddess, and her daughter Persephone. In the *Odyssey* Demeter is mentioned only once, when Calypso complains because Zeus has made it apparent that only he has the right to mortals for sexual purposes.

---

[10] *Od. XXIII*: 213–214, 225–230.
[11] Ibid., 231.

> Thus too, when fair-tressed Demeter, yielding to her pas-
> sion, lay in love with Iasion in the thrice-plowed fallow
> land.[12]

This is hardly the mother goddess we have come to expect from
Bachofen's or Neumann's descriptions, or the mother described
in the *Homeric Hymn to Demeter*. Her daughter from the Hymn,
Persephone, is mentioned in the *Odyssey* as you would expect,
in Books X and XI, when Odysseus is instructed to visit the
Underworld. In Book X, "dread" Persephone, ἐπαινῆς Πέρσε-
φονης, is mentioned five times, three with the appellation
"dread" affixed.[13] In Book XI she makes six appearances.[14] The
first mention is when Odysseus is still far from the dead, and Persephone remains a force to be dreaded. Apart from one mention
of her as the daughter of Zeus, the other four appellations are as
"august" or "noble" Persephone, which denotes her power and
position in the underground realm. As in the *Iliad*, the citings of
Demeter and Persephone do not link in any clear manner with
the *Homeric Hymn to Demeter*.

> But it is only justice to remember that Homer was neither a
> theologian nor a mythographer. . . . Though, as Plato put
> it, Homer had educated all Greece, he had composed his
> poems for a specific audience: the members of a military
> and feudal aristocracy. . . . But since he was not writing a
> treatise on mythology, he did not record all the mythologi-
> cal themes that were in circulation in the Greek world. . . .
> Concerning all that could be called the nocturnal, chtho-
> nian, funereal side of Greek religion and mythology,
> Homer says next to nothing.[15]

Demeter is not represented as the mother Goddess, and Odysseus' own mother Anticleia is only encountered when Odysseus
visits Persephone's realm. There he undergoes the trial of being
unable to comfort the mother who gave birth to him, and of

---

[12] *Od.* V:125–127.

[13] *Od.* X:491, 494, 509, 534, 564.

[14] *Od.* XI 47, 213, 217, 226, 386, 635.

[15] Eliade, *Myth and Reality*, op. cit., 149.

whose death he was unaware. He must follow the instructions of the Goddess Circe, who has helped him to reach this point. This help by Circe will in fact make him twice-born. Are we able to see the role of Circe as maternal? The answer to this must be in the affirmative if we look at the role played by Circe as she guides Odysseus to the underworld, and Calypso fulfils the same role for his journey home. This rebirth, overseen and expedited by Athene, presents her in a role that seems at odds with the vengeful role she plays in the *Iliad*. In the *Odyssey* we see her in the role of polis goddess, so named by Kitto, and this is a much earlier, more chthonic, representation of her. Karl Kerényi makes the same point as Kitto, linking Athene and Hera with the role of polis goddess.[16] Kerényi also points to the darker side of Athene, citing some of the tales associated with her worship.[17] He enlarges on the stories of Aglauros and Iodama, pointing to the duality of nature Athene must show as a mother goddess functioning in a paternalistic system.

> Aglauros and Iodama, the sacrificed, slain, annihilated—but nevertheless living—represent the one aspect of the Goddess that stands over against the other aspect called "Pandrosos" among the sisters of Aglauros but can also have the names "Pallas" or "Nike" or "Victory" . . . Neither of the two poles can exist without the other; always the two together, in their opposition, are Pallas Athene.[18]

Eliade may have grounds for saying that Homer does not foreground the chthonic at least in the *Iliad*, but I do not think that

[16] Kerényi, op. cit., 15:
The cultic places of Athene belong to the peaks of a wider realm, not only feminine and not only inclusive of married life. They exist mostly as shrines of a fortress and city Goddess. This too is a heritage from pre-Greek times. The early history of Athene has been traced back as far as the armed Protectress of the lords of Mycenaean times and beyond that, though somewhat summarily, to the serpent-holding Protectress of the Minoan palaces on Crete.

[17] Ibid., 54:
One such maiden appeared in the Athenian story of Aglauros, who was a being in between the Great Goddess and one of her human servants. The cited festival of the washing of the cultic image, the Plynteria, was associated with her death.

[18] Ibid., 55.

can be said regarding the *Odyssey*. On the contrary, these levels of understanding, these two opposing poles, the duality of birth and death which women and the Goddess represent, are apparent in that poem, and it is this understanding to which Blake is responding in the Arlington Court tempera. As Raine says of Blake's painting:

> Behind him, and still unseen by Odysseus, stands Athena, depicted not with helmet and gorgon-shield, but as the Divine Wisdom.[19]

This is not the aegis-bearing warrior goddess from the *Iliad* but the female in the role of protector and instructor, the mother who leads her children. But she is also the bringer of death, and the Loathly Bride who empowers Odysseus, giving him "the Glory and the Fortune [under] which he operates."[20] The role of Athene can be our guide to understanding this, as she is Odysseus's guide in the poem and the painting.

In Raine's book *Blake and Tradition* the chapter called "The Sea of Time and Space" deals with what is one of Blake's finest paintings: "the tempera discovered at Arlington Court in 1949 and provisionally entitled "The Sea of Time and Space" or "The Cycle of the Life of Man."[21] Raine discusses the influence of Greek thought upon Blake, his resistance to that influence, and finally, in this painting, his acceptance.[22] The painting was completed six years before his death, when Blake himself had been through most of his life cycle, and it clearly shows, through the actions of Odysseus, how Blake saw the role of men and women. Athena

---

[19] Raine, *Blake and Tradition*, op. cit., i., 75.
[20] Coomaraswamy, *Traditional Art and Symbolism*, op. cit., 35.
[21] Raine, op. cit., i., 75.
[22] Ibid:

All the symbols of the Arlington Court painting are familiar to Blake scholars. . . . But in this painting we have clear evidence that Blake invented none of these; it is based upon Porphyry's treatise on Homer's *Cave of the Nymphs*, to which Blake has added details from the *Odyssey* and from Platonic sources. It is a profoundly considered representation of the essentials of Neoplatonism. This work, painted with such evident love, such wealth of symbolic detail, makes it plain that he never forgot a work which had given him his own essential myths.

stands behind Odysseus "pictured as Divine Wisdom" in Raine's words, pointing the way upwards for the embattled traveler. Leucothea is out to sea, ready to catch the scarf thrown by Odysseus. Naiads, groups of winged female figures bearing urns, and the Three Fates are there. The immortals are represented in the sky, where the god resting is in the chariot of the sun, propelled by four horses in turn cared for by four female figures and surrounded by flames of light and spirits. At this moment depicted by Blake, Odysseus has been and will continue to be guided by female gods and royal women as he progresses on his journey. And his goal is the reunion with his wife Penelope, signifying the union of spirit and soul, a reunion Blake personified in his characters Los and Enitharmon.

★★★

The chronological order in the *Iliad* is deliberately not followed by Homer in this poem. We feel we are experiencing Odysseus's life in the same manner as we would our own, with all its mixture of past, present, and future. But Homer needs to tell us what is happening back in Ithaca, and he chooses to do this with the *Telemacheia*. As Knox points out, this allows Homer to introduce the various characters Odysseus will meet on his return home.[23] The surly son, the troubled wife, the loyal nurse, the promiscuous maidservants, the scheming suitors, the Ithacan bard, along with many minor players—all these are introduced to us in these first few books. We, the audience, know just how difficult it has been for Penelope and Telemachus before Odysseus has even left Calypso's island. Telemachus's journey also allows us to meet two successful returnees from the Trojan War: Nestor and Menelaus, and the woman who was its cause, Helen. Knox is of the opinion that Telemachus moves from "provincial diffidence to princely self-confidence" under Athena's tutelage.[24] I would query this "princely self-confidence" displayed by Telemachus. He has been fatherless, but until his grandmother's death and Laertes' withdrawal he had a male role model. His mother and his nurse are the females who have reared him, which was

---

[23] Knox, *Odyssey*, Introduction & Notes, op. cit., 10.
[24] Ibid., 11.

entirely normal for this society, and he is about to step into manhood when this poem commences. This may be the reason he is often unpleasant, if not downright obnoxious, towards his mother. Towards her he shows little respect and, in fact, until Odysseus proves he is his father, the only other person he appears to respect is Eumaeus the swineherd. He is young, untried, and unsure. Does he improve after his voyage and the slaughter of the suitors and their women? One only has to think of the killing of the maidservants. Odysseus has ordered Telemachus, Eumaeus, and Philoetius to make the dishonoring females, fetched by Eurycleia, clean the hall and remove the bodies of the suitors. Then they are to kill them with their swords, but Telemachus has other plans.

> Let it be by no clean death that I take the lives of these women, who on my own head have poured reproaches and on my mother, as they continually slept with the suitors. [25]

The fate of hanging in a row like a line of clothes pegs is theirs, and the fate of Melanthius is even worse. All have betrayed their master and are treated like traitors. But maybe the final battle for Telemachus is not yet over.

Telemachus is unable to stop the suitors from destroying his home because he is not yet a man. As a son, he is unable to cast out his mother without incurring the wrath of the Erinyes, remembering that this is written before the resolution proposed by Aeschylus, and he cannot fight them alone. This is a huge load for any twenty-year-old male to carry, and it is entirely natural that he will blame his mother. When Telemachus meets Athene, disguised as Mentes, she remarks on the family resemblance. Telemachus acknowledges that his mother had told him that he was Odysseus' son, but:

> Therefore, stranger, will I frankly tell you all. My mother says that I am his child; but I do not know this, for never yet did any man know his parentage of his own knowledge. [26]

His response is, of course, truthful because there were then no sci-

---

[25] *Od. XX*: 462–464.
[26] *Od. I*: 214–216.

entific means of identifying the father of the child. It is an odd question for Athene to ask for she knows both his father and mother and, of course, she is a goddess. His answer shows her and us several things. Firstly, there is an apparent slur upon his mother: he only has her word for his parentage. Secondly, his attitude concerning his lineage is that it is unimportant, which demonstrates, thirdly, just how young and insecure he is. This insecurity is played upon by Athene when she wants him to return home.

> Beware lest she carry from your halls some treasure against your will. For you know what sort of a spirit there is in a woman's breast; she wishes to increase the house of the man who marries her, but of her former children and staunch spouse she takes no thought, when once he is dead, and asks no longer concerning them. No, go, and yourself put all your possessions to the charge of whoever of the handmaids seems to you the best, until the gods shall show you your honoured bride.[27]

That he responds so quickly to this apparent dream and thus avoids a return visit to Nestor, demonstrates how little he knows or respects his mother.

Disguised as Mentes, a father figure, Athene is an audience for Telemachus's complaints regarding the suitors and his mother's inability to control them. She bolsters his courage, instructs him on how he is to handle his situation, including sailing off in search of news of his father, what to do if he hears of his father's death, and how another son avenged his father's death—comparing Orestes' situation and his own. She tells him that if he is the son of Odysseus and Penelope, then he possesses the courage and sense to make this journey, and urges him not to cling to his boyhood. Although appearing as a male, Athene plays a maternal role with Telemachus, praising his looks and stressing that he is more than capable of handling the situation. With Athene providing the following wind, the ship sets sail and Telemachus commences his passage from childhood to manhood. Athene has done all in her power to protect Telemachus, bolstering his intent

[27] *Od.XV*:19–26.

where necessary, and the courage of his companions. She has also prevented the wrath of his enemies. We have not yet seen the fiery goddess of the *Iliad*.

★★★

But what of the successful return of the combatants described by Knox? Nestor, the grand old man of the *Iliad*, is surrounded by his sons and appears to be happy in his life. But there is no mention of a mother or wife when we meet him, not even the female companion who warmed his bed in the *Iliad*. And the other successful returnees, Menelaus and Helen, represent a far from ideal pair. Menelaus shows grief for Odysseus's failure to return and would have had him live with him in order that they tell each other stories of the battles that had for so many years consumed their lives. When we meet Helen, she again names herself as "shameless." The self-deprecation Helen uses to describe her behavior in Troy is not even noticed by her husband. It is surely an uncommon thing for a wife to call herself shameless, and yet there is no response. As in the *Iliad*, Helen's remarks about herself and her behavior—which after all had caused the deaths of so many—are treated as commonplace. Instead, Menelaus continues the conversation concerning Telemachus' resemblance to his father.

Are we able to see the mother figure in Helen? She has one daughter, Hermione, "who had the beauty of golden Aphrodite." She is skilled in her feminine crafts, still beautiful and surrounded by luxury, but maternal is not an appellation for Helen. As all who sit at the feast table had been stricken by grief, remembering those lost in that war, Helen instills a drug to make them forget their grief. She had learnt this skill in Egypt, from Polydamna.

> At once she cast into the wine of which they were drinking a drug to quiet all pain and strife, and bring forgetfulness of every ill. Whoever should drink this down, when it is mingled in the bowl, would not in the course of that day let a tear fall down his cheeks, no, not though his mother and father should lie down dead, or though before his face men should slay with the sword his brother or dear son and his own eyes behold it.[28]

[28] *Od. IV*:220–226.

One has a vision of Menelaus, whenever he is feeling a little down in the mouth, being doctored with Helen's potions, and all is bearable again. Their marriage and shared life speaks more of endurance than mutual love and is in very sharp contrast with the reunion of Odysseus and Penelope.

Helen then tells of her encounter with Odysseus while she was still entranced by Paris, when he had disguised himself and entered the city of Troy to discover the strength of their defences. Helen was able to penetrate the disguise and help Odysseus, for her Aphroditean longing for Paris had been replaced by a yearning for home. Menelaus then continues the saga as he politely excuses Helen's betrayal of her fellow countrymen. Odysseus's plan to make a wooden horse and infiltrate the defences of Troy was nearly brought undone by Helen calling to all the fighters inside, "likening your voice to the voices of the wives of all the Argives."[29] Helen, Queen of Sparta, is an image of womanhood who, if compared with Penelope, lacks moral fibre. Her libidinous behavior has caused the death of thousands, and yet she presides, with all her accoutrements of wealth, beside the man she had first betrayed for love and whom she very nearly betrayed to death. As an image of womanhood she does little to inspire respect, and one must question the intelligence of her partner, although this lack of perception regarding the female sex seems to be a family characteristic as we consider her sister, Clytemnestra. This may be "the ideal vision of the hero's return," as Knox says, but it is an Iliadic ideal and presented in order that the contrast is immediately known. Homer is, I think, educating his audience to a differing vision of the relationships between men and women to that shown in the *Iliad*.

★★★

Penelope presents that change in relationships, and a contrast to Helen. In the *Telemacheia* the audience learns of her grief, her beleaguerment, and her solutions. When we first meet Penelope she has been chided by her son for her tears and sent to her rooms. Penelope's role as mother is circumscribed by her undefined role in that society. She is not yet a widow but neither

---

[29] Ibid., 279.

is she a wife. The laws of hospitality prevent her and Telemachus from throwing out the suitors who pursue her. Several things occur in this passage. Telemachus, emboldened and supported by Athene's mothering, is able to stand up to both the suitors and his mother. Penelope, facing for the first time the loss of her child as well as the loss of her husband, retires to her chamber to weep.

> She then, seized with wonder, went back to her chamber, for she laid to her heart the wise saying of her son. Up to her upper chamber she went with her handmaids, and then wept for Odysseus, her dear husband, until grey-eyed Athene cast sweet sleep upon her eyelids.[30]

Here Athene mothers the mother.

In defence of the outrageous behavior by the suitors, Antinous seeks to lay the blame on Penelope, "who is clever above all women," and he describes how she has deferred the decision to marry for three years, weaving and unweaving the shroud for Laertes. This, the fourth year, has seen this cunning come to naught as she has been betrayed by one of her serving women and the shroud is now finished. But through the words of Antinous we see a side of Penelope that confirms her position as a wily Queen of a wily King. Those wiles were demonstrated as she performed that most feminine of tasks, weaving. Penelope, producing something from nothing, weaves a shroud for her father-in-law, Laertes, to stay the pursuit by the suitors. But she then engages in the unfeminine act of destroying what she has made. Antinous tells Telemachus that he must force his mother to make a decision or his estate will be devoured by them.

Penelope's reaction to the news of her son's trip to Pylos and Lacedaemon, where he seeks to gain information concerning his father's fate, is overwhelming grief: her fear that she has lost her husband is now coupled with the fear that she will lose her son. Penelope wants the news of Telemachus's absence sent to Laertes in the hope that he will be able to forestall the plans of the suitors, but Eurycleia soothes her grief, urging her to pray to Pallas Athene and not to trouble the old man. Athene hears

---

[30] *Od.*I:360–364.

Penelope's prayer and, in disguise, tells her that Telemachus will arrive home safely while the suitors prepare a ship to waylay Telemachus on his voyage home. Athene, disguised as Ipththime, Icarius's daughter and Penelope's sister, soothes and mothers her. When she is sleeping peacefully, Athene returns to Olympus and adopts a more aggressive stance towards her fellow gods. She reminds them that Odysseus is still not home. Zeus tells her that she is trying to drum up needless support, for they have already agreed on a plan of action. With this, Athene is sent to take care of Telemachus and Hermes to inform Calypso of Zeus's decree. Hermes is to give Calypso instructions concerning

> the return of steadfast Odysseus, that he may return with guidance neither of gods nor of mortal men, but that on a stoutly bound raft, suffering woes, he may come on the twentieth day to deep-soiled Scheria, the land of the Phaeacians.[31]

On his return he finds that the suitors have broken one of the foremost rules of Greek hospitality by the unbridled imposition of their demands upon Odysseus's household.[32] Odysseus, as beg-

---

[31] *Od.V*:31–35.

[32] Knox, *Odyssey*, Introduction & Notes, op. cit., 44 Knox puts forward a very good argument for the *Odyssey* signaling the end of this generosity to strangers with Zeus's decision, which allows Poseidon to wall off Phaeacia:

> This is the end of the great Phaeacian tradition of hospitality and help for the stranger and wayfarer. This action of Zeus casts a disturbing light on the relation between human ideals and divine conduct. If there is one stable moral criterion in the world of the *Odyssey*, it is the care taken by the powerful and well-to-do of strangers, wanderers and beggars. This code of hospitality is the one universally recognized morality. And its divine enforcer, so all mortals believe, is Zeus himself, Zeus *xeinios*, protector of stranger and suppliant.

I am reminded of Blake when he speaks of the reliance of only the senses as a means of control, of enclosure, depriving the individual of the use of intellect:

> They told me that I had five senses to inclose me up,
> And they inclos'd my infinite brain into a narrow circle
> And sunk my heart into the Abyss, a red, round globe, hot burning,
> Till all from life I was obliterated and erased. *K.* 191, *VDA.*2:31

This is what occurs to Phaeacia, the kingdom of the mind with its wonderful ships that fly like arrows of thought. It is now enclosed, cut off from mortals seeking help.

gar and on Athene's command, tests the generosity of the suitors at the table. Odysseus displays some disinclination to believe the worst of them. Antinous dispels that doubt. On hearing of this maltreatment, Penelope summons Odysseus to her chambers that she may demonstrate true hospitality to the beggar, and this he promises to do on the setting of the sun. But Odysseus sees Penelope before that, as she is stirred—by Athene—to visit the hall where the suitors are feasting, to chastise Telemachus. Odysseus has defeated a rival beggar for a position in the hall and listens with admiration to her speech to the suitors:

> Those who wish to woo a lady of worth and the daughter of a rich man and vie with one another, these themselves bring cattle and fat sheep, and banquet for the friends of the bride, and give to her glorious gifts; they do not devour the livelihood of another without atonement.[33]

Although Penelope is the promised reward, Odysseus is extremely happy to see his wife's shrewdness, as she accepts their gifts and retires to her chamber. Once again, with the limited powers that she has, Penelope has lived up to her reputation. In compliance with Odysseus's instructions when he left for Troy— that is, to take a husband if he does not return—she solves the problem of the suitors by setting them a challenge to win her hand. She has discussed this with Odysseus, in the role of beggar, and her solution is formidable. The challenge the suitors must meet is to string Odysseus's bow. She will marry the one who is able to shoot an arrow through the line of twelve axes and thus protect her son's inheritance. Penelope is a remarkable match for her husband, resourceful and cunning, so much so that even though her desire to know her husband again is so great, she will not accept him until he as well has passed her test. That this provokes Telemachus we have already seen, but it angers Odysseus: "Woman, truly this is a bitter word that you have spoken. Who has set my bed elsewhere?"[34] This is a little unfair, considering that he did not completely trust her. His enquiries of Telemachus

---

[33] *Od. XVIII*:276–280.
[34] Ibid., 183–184.

on his arrival at Eumaeus's hut were directed to finding out if he had any siblings. Penelope has been alone for over twenty years, during which time she has looked after his property, including herself, to the best of her ability. Why should she believe this stranger with her husband's face when it could be a god in disguise? It is merely further proof of her very good sense.

★★★

When Odysseus relinquished his hold on those things of the sense bestowed by Calypso and surrendered himself to the chaos of the sea, he lands, naked, on Scheria, the land of the Phaeacians, ruled by King Alcinous, descendant of the "great-hearted Nausithous." Reborn from the sea, which has become as amniotic fluid, with Ino as midwife and Athene as mother, he is ready to start the process of rebirth. All his previous trials and pleasures have been washed away by immersion and submersion in this fluid world of Poseidon. He has landed in this place, the Kingdom of the Phaeacia, far from anywhere, a land whose sailors man ships with minds, setting them flying like arrows of thought.

The next part of Odysseus's journey commences under the auspices of a nubile female, Nausicaa. He is naked and addresses her with high praise:

> But that man in his turn is blessed in heart above all others, who shall prevail with his gifts of wooing and lead you to his home. For never yet have my eyes looked upon a mortal such as you, whether man or woman; awe holds me as I look on you.[35]

We may dismiss this as hyperbole on the part of Odysseus, but why marriage? Does he mention marriage because this is the reason for his odyssey, thinking, hoping that he also will be a man "blessed in heart above all others?" Or, is it merely because she is young and unattached? Homer has drawn our attention to marriage here because of its significance, adding force to Odysseus's renunciation of immortality in favor of a return to his own marriage.

Without the assistance of Nausicaa and Athene, Odysseus would still be asleep under the leaves. To progress further, Odys-

---

[35] *Od.* VI:158–161.

seus must ask for aid from another female, Queen Arete. Odysseus sets off for the palace shrouded in mist, sent by Athene. She, disguised as a young girl, meets Odysseus at the gates of the city and offers to take him to the palace. As Athene does this, she also tells him of the history of the royal family who descend from Poseidon and Periboea. She stresses the importance of the relationship between Arete and Alcinous: "Her Alcinous made his wife, and honored her as no other woman on earth is honored."[36] This is a momentous statement concerning the marital relationship in light of the married couples we have seen in both the *Iliad* and *Odyssey.* She is a woman whose judgement is so acute that she is called upon to settle quarrels "even if they are men." Surely we have here a wonderful example of the acceptance of Blake's contrarieties. Arete, female, and Alcinous, male, are opposing forces which honor the other's capabilities and are the necessary correlative. This is a *hieros gamos;* or in Blake's words, one thinks of the other as "my garden of delight," and the other is "the spirit in the garden."

Still shrouded by Athene's mist, Odysseus enters the palace and strides through the hall, past the Phaeacian leaders and counsellors, direct to Queen Arete. When this happens the mist dissolves and all in the hall are wonder-struck at Odysseus's appearance. Odysseus grasps the knees of Queen Arete and "there and then the wondrous mist melted from him."

> Arete, daughter of godlike Rhexenor, to your husband and to your knees have I come suppliant after many toils, and to these banqueters, too, to whom may the gods grant happiness in life, and may each of them hand down to his children the wealth in his halls, and the dues of honor which the people have given him. But grant me speedy conveyance, that I may come to my native land, and quickly; for it is a long time that I have been suffering woes far from my people.[37]

This image of Odysseus, supplicant at the knees of a woman, is a powerful one. From her he begs for a passage home to mortal

---

[36] *Od.VII*:66–67.
[37] Ibid., 146–152.

life. From her daughter he has already been given the chance for that life to resume. And let us not forget the importance of the care shown by Athene for Odysseus. She is always there, protecting, ensuring that his appearance is god-like in any circumstance. Arete and Alcinous welcome Odysseus and extend their hospitality to this stranger. At the feasting, Demodocus sings of the net that caught an unfaithful wife. Hephaestus, the master craftsman, has ensnared his wife, Aphrodite, engaged in cuckolding him with Ares and calls on the gods to bear witness. Hephaestus has asked all the gods to witness this, but the "goddesses stayed behind for shame."[38] Although Hephaestus is devastated, Hermes and Apollo find it comic and there are asides about whether they would chance being caught if they could enjoy Aphrodite. Poseidon and the absent goddesses are not amused, however, at this farce.[39] Hephaestus's marriage to Charis, in the *Iliad*—which demonstrates gentleness and mutual respect—is ignored here. And the person responsible for this is the domineering mother, Hera. There are echoes of the duel scene in the *Iliad* here as if there is a necessity to lighten the sorrows that have happened, but the cuckolded husband in the *Odyssey* is in control and the cuckolders shamed. It is of course a very sharp contrast to the *hieros gamos* displayed by Arete and Alcinous.

After the feasting, the games and dancing, the gift giving, Odysseus is ready to return home far wealthier than when he landed, naked, on Phaeacia's shores. But he has gained far more than silver swords. Even in receiving these gifts a woman tells him how to secure them and another female has shown him the means by which he may do this. Arete directs Odysseus to bind the chest containing his gifts: "for fear some one rob you of your goods on the way, when later on you are lying in sweet sleep, as you travel in the black ship."[40] With the gifts securely wrapped and tied with a cunning knot that queenly Circe had once taught him'—yet another helpful female—Odysseus is ready to depart. But when the final meal is served and Demodocus sings of the

---

[38] *Od. VIII*:324.
[39] Slater, op. cit., 194.
[40] *Od. VIII*:444–445.

wooden horse that gained entry to Troy, Odysseus is no longer able to hide his tears:

> But the heart of Odysseus was melted and tears wet his cheeks beneath his eyelids. And as a woman wails and throws herself upon her dear husband, who has fallen in front of his city and his people, seeking to ward off from his city and his children the pitiless day; and as she beholds him dying and gasping for breath, she clings to him and shrieks aloud, while the foe behind her beat her back and shoulders with their spears, and lead her away to captivity to bear toil and woe, while with most pitiful grief her cheeks are wasted—so did Odysseus let fall pitiful tears from beneath his brows.[41]

What is evoked here is the image of Andromache after the death of Hector, when she realizes that all she feared will now come to pass. Homer has compared this powerful warrior to a woman. Were his listeners shocked? Are we shocked? Is he saying that despite the physical attributes that separate man and woman, nevertheless they are the same? If this is so, then this poem is about recognizing the human being at its fullest: male and female, spirit and soul, are one. It is a tale of the return home of someone lost, as we are all lost. Alcinous is the only person to notice Odysseus's grief. He calls on the bard to stop, as his guest is clearly overcome with grief, and asks Odysseus to identify himself and whence he came. Odysseus is now in a place of safety and knows that he will soon arrive home in one of these magical ships. Now he may tell his tale.

Alcinous foretells the fate that awaits the Kingdom of Phaeacia because they have assisted this mortal who has offended Poseidon. A fate told to him by his father, King Nausithous. Phaeacia, ruled by twelve nobles, the twelve months, and one king, the year itself; whose inhabitants are sailors who sail their ships safely across any ocean to the ends of the earth; black ships, black as the night, in which the passenger lies asleep. And the final fate that awaits Phaeacia is to have its port surrounded by a huge moun-

---

[41] *Od. VIII*: 521–531.

tain put there as punishment by Poseidon. No longer will their swift black ships fly across Poseidon's realm with the speed of thought. Knowing this is their end, why does Alcinous continue to help Odysseus? This enclosing of the kingdom of the mind is like the ossification described by Blake in the creation of Urizen, or man's reasoning power:

> Forgetfulness, dumbness, necessity, in chains of the mind
>   lock'd up,
> In fetters of ice shrinking, disorganiz'd, rent from Eternity,
> Los beat on his fetters & [pour'd del.] heated his furnaces,
> And pour'd iron sodor & sodor of brass.
> Restless the immortal inchain'd, heaving dolorous,
> Anguish'd unbearable till a roof, shaggy wild, inclos'd
> In an orb his fountain of thought.[42]

Blake continues with the symbol of constructing a bony carapace for reason. The enclosure of the kingdom of the mind is an idea to which both poets have responded.

Urged on by Alcinous, Odysseus commences the tale of his journeying. He begins by giving his name: "I am Odysseus, son of Laertes, known to all men for my stratagems, and my fame reaches the heavens."[43] This statement by Odysseus, naming his parentage and abilities, is very similar to the one he makes to the Cyclops, Polyphemus. But the statement made to Polyphemus sets up the terrible events that follow as he undergoes, quite literally, a sea change.

> Cyclops, if any one of mortal men shall ask you about the
> shameful blinding of your eye, say that Odysseus, the sacker
> of cities, blinded it, the son of Laertes, whose home is in Ith-
> aca.[44]

On both occasions Odysseus has been "Nobody" before making his proclamation, but there is a very great difference in the person speaking to Alcinous. When Odysseus makes his defiant statement to Polyphemus, he does so after becoming a non-per-

---

[42] *K.303, FZ.3:211.*
[43] *Od. IX:19–20.*
[44] Ibid., 502–505.

son in order to escape death. Once he is safe from death, he then reverts to the warrior he had been in the *Iliad,* with all the bravado that entails. The non-person he has become when speaking to Alcinous has come after losing his entire persona. In order to achieve this nothingness he has had to undergo many trials until he arrives at Phaeacia, naked, having nothing, to be reborn. Odysseus has become another person.

He tells the tale of how he has become the man he now is, and in that telling we meet all the females who have aided that growth: Leucothea, Calypso, Circe, Nausicaa, Arete, and above all others, Athene. Others have attempted to hinder his and his crew's progress: the Laestrygonian King's daughter, the Sirens, Scylla and Charybdis. On his journey to the Underworld Odysseus, after he has first honored his dead companion, then Teiresias, and next his mother, there is a parade of females sent by Persephone. Homer is emphasizing the feminine at this point. Again, what we, and Odysseus, have seen in the realm of Persephone is a softening of the values extolled in the *Iliad.* Women are presented to him before the men. Heroic men are presented as overwhelmed by the fury of women, in the case of Agamemnon, and regretting their heroic stance and death, in the case of Achilles. Both Agamemnon and Achilles enquire about their sons as their true source of immortality. Above all else there is pity and compassion shown by both male and female. We see it clearly in Odysseus's mother, Anticleia. But Odysseus shows pity towards Achilles, Great Ajax, Agamemnon and his mother. That other aspect of the feminine, death, is represented by Persephone, and it is clear that she rules both men and women. But his journey home is almost complete. Alcinous prepares a farewell feast and Nausicaa bids him farewell:

> Farewell, stranger, and hereafter even in your native land may you remember me, for to me first you owe the price of your life.[45]

Odysseus acknowledges this debt in his answer: "I will there, too, pray to you as to a god all my days, for you, maiden, have given

[45] *Od.VIII*: 461–462.

me life."[46] Again, Homer is emphasizing the importance of the feminine.

Once aboard the ship the oarsmen commence their work, Odysseus succumbs to sleep and in this magical sleep sets sail for Ithaca:

> Thus she sped on swiftly and cut through the waves of the sea, bearing a man wise as the gods are wise, one who in time past had suffered many griefs at heart in passing through wars of men and the grievous waves; but now he slept in peace, forgetful of all that he had suffered.[47]

The ship enters the safe harbour of Phorcys, on Ithaca, which contains the cave with two entrances, one for mortals and one for immortals. Beaching the ship, the crew unload Odysseus, still sleeping, and his treasure, leaving it neatly piled near the olive tree. Then the Phaeacians commence their trip home.

★★★

Odysseus is now in the place depicted by Blake in the painting "The Sea of Time and Space." Raine's description of the painting allows us to see how accurately he has used his sources:

> In Blake's painting the figure on the sea-verge is Odysseus, newly landed on his native shore, in the cove of the sea god Phorcys, close to the Cave of the Nymphs. His dark, clever face is a highly convincing "vision" of that wary-wise Greek. . . . Behind him, and still unseen by Odysseus, stands Athena, depicted not with helmet and gorgon-shield, but as the Divine Wisdom. . . . Odysseus is in the act of throwing something out to sea, with his face averted. What has he thrown? Out at sea a nymph or goddess has caught a scarf-like wreath. . . . She is Leucothea, or Ino, who lent Odysseus her sea-girdle by which he came safe ashore—not on the coast of Ithaca but on the shore of Phaeacia. Blake has combined the two accounts of the hero's coming safe to land.[48]

Raine then discusses the other figures in the painting, naiads, a

---

[46] Ibid., 467–468.
[47] *Od. XIII*:88–92.
[48] Raine, *Blake and Tradition*, op. cit., i., 75–76.

pair of lovers, winged female figures, and other nymphs weaving on looms, Phorcys and the three Fates. Raine puts forward the suggestion that the three Fates were taken from the Orphic *Hymn to the Fates* and were included by Blake because of the association with the flow of water. The predominance of the female figure in this painting is a reflection of the importance of the female in the poem itself. Blake has recognized this perhaps by his knowledge of Porphyry, as Raine suggests, or perhaps through his own knowledge of the balance between male and female achieved by Homer in the *Odyssey*. There are males, the immortals, Phorcys, "the old man of the sea," and Helios, the Sun God. There is a male participant in the pair of lovers, and Odysseus himself to represent the mortal males. The choice of Helios is interesting. Does Blake choose him because Odysseus is waking up after the night's journey? Or does it tie in with the power wielded by the female goddesses over the dawning of the sun? I am reminded of the control imposed by Hera, in the *Iliad*, when Zeus ordered the fighting to continue until the sun went down. Hera, protecting her men as a mother would her children, forced Helios to bed. Athene, protecting the couple who had endured so much before their reunion, will order Dawn to stay her rising until they have had time together after Penelope finally recognizes Odysseus.

What occurs after this is Odysseus's resumption of his mortal self as King of Ithaca, but only after the "stripping off of the ragged garments of mortality."[49] All the events that will take place after Odysseus identifies himself to Telemachus may be read as the final victory for the hero as he rids his home of those invaders who seek his wife's hand. Or, we may read the death of the suitors as a further shedding of undesirable aspects of Odysseus; and, indeed, we may read his odyssey as a ridding of the most undesirable aspects of his nature: sloth, pride, avarice, greed—aspects of our human nature that are often companions for life if the life lived is unexamined. This is in line with the read-

---

[49] Op. cit. Raine draws a parallel between Taylor's symbol "and the many instances in Blake's writings . . . to the beggar's rags of which Odysseus divested himself when he returned to Ithaca."

ing Raine attributes to Blake and his painting, the debt he owed to the Neoplatonists.

Penelope has been a faithful wife, constant and true. There have not been many ways in which she can best or control the suitors, but what there have been she has found. The comparison with Clytemnestra and Helen is striking. First and foremost she is a mother, and that role has led her to seek a solution in order that Telemachus will not suffer any more from the depredations of the suitors. When younger, Telemachus required her to be there. Now he is a man she will leave, although leaving is not her desire, and indeed she prays for her own death if a suitor succeeds. Of course it is Odysseus who is successful, and after proving his identity it is Odysseus whom she welcomes home. Of the three marriages we have seen, the marriage of Helen and Menelaus is strikingly different. Arete and Alcinous closely represent the idea of sacred marriage. The marriage of Penelope and Odysseus seems to follow in that same pattern while Helen and Menelaus are not even close to that ideal. Remembering Johnson's criteria for a "successful" love story, one must say that Penelope and Odysseus are exemplars of that ideal.

Neither the *Iliad* nor the *Odyssey* emphasize Blake's feminine attribute of pity. Apart from Achilles' reception of Priam there is little pity shown in the *Iliad* except earlier, when ransom redeemed a life—and that was a purchased pity. In the *Odyssey*, Odysseus shows pity towards those souls in the underworld, but no pity is shown to the suitors or maidservants, particularly on the part of Athene. In both epics the female gods are adamantine against those in their path. Nevertheless we as the audience feel pity towards the protagonists of both epics. Aristotle says that:

> Tragedy, then, is mimesis of an action, which is elevated, complete, and of magnitude; in language embellished by distinct forms in its sections; employing the mode of enactment, not narrative; and through pity and fear accomplishing the catharsis of such emotions.[50]

[50] Aristotle, XXIII, *Poetics*, trans. Halliwell, 1995, Cambridge, Mass, Harvard University Press, 1449b:23–28.

Aristotle is speaking of plays here, but the Homeric epics are also "tragedy," if by tragedy we expect loss, suffering, pain, and death to occur, and the catharsis that follows on our feeling pity. In Aristotle's outline for invoking catharsis, he moves from tragedy to epic:

> Moreover, epic should encompass the same types as tragedy, namely simple, complex, character-based, rich in suffering; it has the same components . . . for it requires reversals, recognitions, and scenes of suffering, as well as effective thought and diction, all of which Homer was the first to employ, and employed proficiently.[51]

Of Homer's epics, Aristotle says, "yet these poems are structured as well as could be."[52] Pity, as a spiritual or civilizing emotion, has played no great role in this society except, if we can accept Aristotle's dictum, in the cathartic effect it has on its audience. With Odysseus however there does appear to be an inkling that this may be changing as well. Overall and more importantly, the reader must feel that the odyssey which is our life is something that must be undertaken with care and insight if the goal of home is to be reached.

Odysseus shows restraint when he is victorious against the suitors. This is a very different man from the one who proclaimed his status to Polyphemus. He silences Eurycleia when she "made ready to raise the cry of celebration"[53] on seeing the strewn bodies of the suitors. His words to her are:

> In your own heart rejoice, old woman, but refrain yourself and do not cry out aloud: an unholy thing is it to boast over slain men. These men have the fate of the gods destroyed and their own reckless deeds, for they honoured no one of men upon the earth, high or low, whoever came among them; therefore by their wanton folly they brought on themselves a shameful death.[54]

---

[51] Op. cit., 1459b: 8–14.
[52] Ibid., 1461b: 36, 1462a: 1–3.
[53] Od. XXII: 408.
[54] Ibid., 411–416.

It is pity that Odysseus displays here, acknowledging human frailty. These men who, nevertheless, were the children of parents, thought they could flout divine and human rules with impunity and they died shameful deaths. As Odysseus's companions, unable to control their physical appetites, were punished by death, so too the suitors must die. But we are not to boast in their deaths but rather to feel pity that these lives were wasted.

The *Odyssey* is the mirror image to the *Iliad*. Odysseus is held captive by Circe and Calypso in the same manner as the women trophies are in the *Iliad*. Like them, he is unable to escape his fate. Like them, he wishes to be elsewhere, and not to be merely a sexual object. Unlike them, he is offered immortality and ageless youth, which he refuses, tactfully:

> Mighty goddess, do not be angry with me for this. I know very well myself that wise Penelope is less impressive to look upon than you in looks and stature, for she is a mortal, while you are immortal and ageless. But even so I wish and long day in and day out to reach my home, and to see the day of my return.[55]

Zeus has intervened on Odysseus's behalf to free him from this bondage, something that does not occur for the Iliadic women; but it is Athene's compassion for his sorrow that causes the intervention. Our first encounter with Odysseus is when Calypso relates to him Zeus's instructions.

> Him she found sitting on the shore, and his eyes were never dry of tears, and his sweet life was ebbing away, as he grieved for his return, for the nymph no longer pleased him. By night indeed he would sleep by her side perforce in the hollow caves, unwilling beside the willing nymph, but by day he would sit on the rocks and the sands, racking his heart with tears and groans and griefs, and he would look out over the unresting sea, shedding tears.[56]

Calypso also tells Odysseus he will undergo more travail before he reaches home. His mourning for Penelope, "for whom you

---

[55] *Od.* V: 215–220.
[56] Ibid., 151–158.

long day in and day out,"[57] is incomprehensible to her, as is his refusal of immortality. Odysseus's desire to share a mortal life with a mortal companion, Penelope, his wife, is at odds with the warrior culture described in the *Iliad*. The Iliadic marriage does not share this concept of *hieros gamos,* a concept we have seen personified in the marriage of Arete and Alcinous. The Odyssean marriage is an attempt to realize this ideal.

Penelope's ability to thwart the suitors is also a mirroring of what has occurred with Paris and Helen. Paris and the suitors break the rules of Greek hospitality. The difference between these two attempts is that one is successful—Paris escapes with Helen—and one is not. Penelope is able to maintain a presence in her own home and, by trickery or cunning, prevent the suitors from complete demolishment of the home before the return of Odysseus. One is the cause of the Trojan War, and the other— providing Odysseus completes the tasks set by Tiresias—will enjoy "sleek old age" with her husband. Helen rejoins her husband, Menelaus, but this is a contrast between marriages. Menelaus is still hankering after the glory days of war and is kept in line with medication whenever necessary. Or, perhaps, in the knowledge that if he stays married to Helen he will enjoy better treatment after death.

Marriage itself is presented differently in the *Odyssey* and this is very apparent in the family line of Odysseus. When, in Book XVI, a disguised Odysseus meets his son, Telemachus, he questions him about help from his siblings. Telemachus replies:

> for such is the manner in which the son of Cronus has made our house run in but a single line. As his only son did Arceisius beget Laertes, as his only son again did his father beget Odysseus, and Odysseus begot me as his only son, and left me in his halls, and had no joy of me.[58]

Coupled with the words of the nurse, Eurycleia, in Book I, we begin to see a contrast with the marriages of the line of Arceisius

---

[57] *Od. V:* 210.
[58] *Od. XVI:* 117–120.

with others presented in the *Iliad*. Eurycleia's role is of importance and this is her story:

> This Eurycleia, daughter of Ops, son of Peisenor, was a servant of sterling character whom Laertes had procured at his own cost long ago, when she was still a girl, for the price of twenty oxen. He had treated her in his home with all the deference that is paid to a loyal wife, though for fear of his lady's displeasure he had respected her bed.[59]

Eurycleia is a slave, but a slave with some position within the family, and because of his wife's feelings she is not used sexually by the man who purchased her. This of course ensures that there will be only one son born to Laertes, as his wife had no more children. Odysseus, unlike the other Greeks, does not appear to have any female prizes from the Trojan War on his ships. He may well have intended to bring some of the Cicones' wives, for they were divided equally among the ships, but that was prevented by the Cicones themselves. Therefore Telemachus will be the one son from his union with Penelope. The contrast between this and the begetting that fills Priam's halls is stark. That the Trojans are foreign, sybaritic, and effete and therefore worthy of defeat is also implied in the *Iliad*. But the Iliadic Greeks do not compare favorably with this Odyssean family. Agamemnon is married and returns with at least one prize, Cassandra. Nestor is accompanied by someone he had won with his skill in battle. Achilles erupts with rage when his prize, Briseis, is removed from him, although he does have an emergency female who takes her place. He is already married and has a son. Menelaus appears to be content with the absent Helen. At the Funeral Games women are given in prizes. This appears to be a very different view towards marriage and the female than that shown in the *Odyssey*, and something Homer wants us to consider. Doherty makes the following statement concerning these poems.

> In the Homeric epics, men are portrayed as the protectors of women, yet they capture the wives and daughters of other

---

[59] Homer, *The Odyssey*, trans. Rieu, 1967, Middlesex, Penguin Books, I:428–433.

men and use them as slaves or concubines; indeed, the possession of such women is considered a mark of high honour.[60]

I do not disagree with this point of view where it concerns the *Iliad*, but the *Odyssey* is a very different story. Far from successfully capturing "wives and daughters of other men," Odysseus has himself been captured. There were no prizes brought back to Ithaca from Troy. It may be no more than the Greek idea of presenting opposites in order to achieve a clearer understanding, and in the next chapter I will look at more of these contraries.

[60] Doherty, op. cit., 35.

PART FOUR

Women's Diverging Roles

7

The Iliadic and Odyssean Divergence

THE ROLE of women in Greek thought diverges into two from the time of the Homeric epics. One branch follows the Iliadic conception, through Hesiod, Aristotle and the poets, Aeschylus down to Euripides. The other shows its colors in the *Odyssey*, the *Homeric Hymn to Demeter*, Parmenides, Plato, and in their esoterica. In his *Works and Days*, Hesiod states that "the tribes of men used to live upon the earth entirely apart from evils."[1] Zeus orders Hephaestus to fashion a beautiful woman, and Athena, Aphrodite, and Hermes each give her certain gifts, as do the lesser goddesses.[2] She is of course Pandora, and in Hesiod's thought it seems that her sex is sufficient cause to allocate to her the blame for all evils in the world.[3] One might ponder why Zeus

---

[1] Hesiod, *Theogony, Works and Days, Testimonia*, ed. & trans. Most, 2006, Cambridge, Harvard University Press, "Works and Days," 90–91.

[2] Ibid., 585–593:

Then, when he had contrived this beautiful evil thing in exchange for that good one, he led her out where the other gods and the human beings were, while she exulted in the adornment of the mighty father's bright-eyed daughter, and wonder gripped the immortal gods and the mortal human beings when they saw the steep deception, intractable for human beings. For from her comes the race of female women: for of her is the deadly race and tribe of women, a great woe for mortals, dwelling with men, no companions of baneful poverty but only of luxury.

[3] Ibid., 93–100:

But the woman removed the great lid from the storage jar with her hands and scattered all its contents abroad—she wrought baneful evils for human beings. Only Anticipation remained there in its unbreakable home under the mouth of the storage jar and did not fly out; for before that could happen she closed the lid of the storage jar, by the plans of the aegis-holder, the cloud-gatherer Zeus.

felt the need to cause this pain for humanity and the answer is that it is his gift in exchange for the Promethean gift of fire.

> To them I shall give in exchange for fire an evil in which they may all take pleasure in their spirit, embracing their own evil.[4]

This is God as Blake's Nobodaddy, the false God of this World.

> Then old Nobodaddy aloft
> Farted & belch'd & cough'd
> And said, "I love hanging & drawing & quartering
> Every bit as well as war & slaughtering.[5]

Aeschylus was born at Eleusis near Athens in 525 BC, and came from a noble family. His trilogy, *The Oresteia*, deals with families of noble birth who are subsequently judged by the demos, as in a democracy. "The Agamemnon" deals with the return from the Trojan War of Agamemnon and his subsequent despatch by his wife, Clytemnestra. "The Choephori," or "The Libation Bearers," is concerned with Orestes slaying his mother, Clytemnestra, and his pursuit by the Erinyes, the Furies. The final play is "The Eumenides," when Orestes and the Furies are judged by the demos, with Athene holding the balance of power. Phillip Vellacott states that Aeschylus wrote these plays "some thirty years after the battle of Marathon, while the new Athenian democracy was bursting into full life."[6] Vellacott, in his introduction, proposes that Aeschylus is representing a transition from the old form of justice to the new, that what we see is a replacement of the Erinyes by the Eumenides. The Erinyes are representative of the old chthonic form of justice, while the Eumenides represent the new, rational and equitable form, which will presumably more readily fit the democratic society for which Aeschylus is writing. This trilogy appears to support democratic rule and the institution of a new form of justice, but Aeschylus's writing appears to

---

[4] Hesiod, op. cit., 57–58.

[5] K.185, *Poems from the Notebook 1793*, 60:9.

[6] Aeschylus, *The Oresteian Trilogy*, trans. Vellacott, 1983, Middlesex, Penguin Books, 15.

undercut both this form of justice and the new democracy. His chorus, when acting as the demos, is portrayed as vacillating and weak, influenced by whomever is more powerful. By contrast, his portrayal of Clytemnestra is strong and savage. If Aeschylus does not think that democratic government is best, perhaps we may also say that his opinion concerning the decision to support matricide is to be questioned. I do not think, however, that Aeschylus is content with this resolution, and that lack of contentment may translate into discontent with the society itself.

In the final play Athene is true to her Iliadic persona. She votes on the masculine side, perhaps because of her birth, although exempting herself from marriage that she may owe no allegiance to a husband. The vote from the citizens is fifty-fifty, as might be expected, and Athene casts the deciding vote. Athene diffuses the anger of the older gods, the Erinyes, and promises them honor in their new state as the Eumenides. And the Eumenides promise Athens a great and glorious future. What is interesting is the singular honor shown to the old gods, the Erinyes/Eumenides, at the conclusion of the play. A procession honoring the feminine goddesses, led by a "reverend troop of elder women, dressed in robes of purple dye,"[7] takes place. They have the right to wear the purple dye, while Agamemnon was incited to slight the gods by walking on a purple carpet. Athene, the goddess of wisdom, is constant to her nature, demonstrating her powers of discernment and appeasement, and it is she who leads the procession honoring the feminine, an honoring that continues with the Panathenaea. But this honoring of the feminine coincides with the loss of recognition for the role of the mother. Clytemnestra, as portrayed by Aeschylus, has slain her husband, a non blood relative, because he has offered their daughter, Iphigenia, as a sacrifice; "He killed her for a charm to stop the Thracian wind."[8] The wrath of the mother regarding her blood relative, her child, is overwhelming in Clytemnestra's speech to the Chorus. She is shown as the person responsible for the planning and execution of her husband,

[7] Aeschylus, *The Eumenides*, op. cit., 1028–1029.
[8] Aeschylus, *Agamemnon*, op. cit., 1417–1418.

with Aegisthus as a mere accessory in complete contrast to the portrayal by Homer. By elevating the position of the mother in the execution of this deed and then relegating her, in the final play, to a mere receptacle, Aeschylus leaves us puzzled.

Aeschylus shows us a world operating under inverted laws, and it is not successful. It is so unsuccessful that one must wonder if he meant us to realize that this is what would happen under democratic rule—that this means of government must rely upon the gods to resolve issues such as have been presented in the plays. That his resolution depends upon divine intervention leads me to believe that he did not approve of democracy, but instead favored a society with a religious basis. Nor do I believe he fully believed in the arguments he places in Apollo's mouth—and therefore we as readers should question them. This is not to say that he would advocate following the path of the Lycians, but nevertheless I do not think the democratic path was his path of choice, nor do I believe he whole-heartedly endorsed the complete dismissal of the female.

Euripides (485–406 BC) is an even stronger indication of the changes in the legend of the mother goddess than Aeschylus, who precedes him by 40 years. Let us consider Euripides' telling of the Bacchantes story, a story in support of the role of Dionysus. Euripides' women are terrifying, possessed females whose maternal instincts are either suppressed by frenzy, revenge, or jealousy. They present the female and the mother in a thoroughly unattractive light. In *The Bacchae* Euripides allows Teiresias to make the following argument to Pentheus, a point that is made by our modern practitioners of hypnosis: no one can be made to do, while in a hypnotic trance or in the thrall of a god, that which is against their moral beliefs. Teiresias makes this point to Pentheus: these women do not have to behave like madwomen just because they are following a god. A maiden will behave with decorum if that is in her nature. Teiresias implores Pentheus to welcome this new god to Thebes and says:

> Dionysos does not, I admit, compel a woman
> to be chaste. Always and in every case
> it is her character and nature that keeps

a woman chaste. But even in the rites of Dionysos
the chaste woman will not be corrupted.[9]

So we must not blame Dionysus for the behavior of Agave when she and Ino rip the arms from her son. The god-given delusion that Agave labors under enables her to join the frenzied Bacchantes who rend her son's body apart. When she carries the trophy of his bloody head back to Thebes she insists it is the head of a young lion. Are we to believe she is exhibiting her true nature, for she cannot do what she is not morally able to do? That women, mothers, sisters, lovers are able to treat their loved ones with this callousness because it is their nature? This is a truly frightening picture of women and motherhood presented by Euripides, and it is not aberrant. This frightening female form is one to which he constantly alludes in his work. We have already seen that this is an aspect of the feminine—*Kolyo, Kālī, the Loathly Bride—but Euripides concentrates only on this aspect of the female. By ignoring or forgetting the balancing aspect of the nurturing female, Euripides, and those who follow, make woman, if not a chilling evil, then a wayward fool.

Pentheus, in his threats to Dionysus and his female followers, at least shows some awareness that they are not occupying their proper place in society. Unfortunately, he uses further displacement as a threat, threatening to sell them as slaves:

> As for these women,
> Your accomplices in making trouble here,
> I shall have them sold as slaves or put to work
> at my looms. That will silence their drums.[10]

They will no longer be loved ones, wives and daughters, but become slaves, either at home or abroad. Agave is most certainly guilty of hubris. She rejoices in her own and her sisters' ability to kill barehanded when in the grip of the god's frenzy. In this, she seeks to place herself in the position of the male. After these exploits Agave asks,

---

[9] Euripides, *Bacchantes,* trans. Arrowsmith, eds. Grene & Lattimore, 1970, Chicago, University of Chicago, 310–318.

[10] Ibid., 512–514.

What are they worth,
your boastings now, and all that uselessness
your armor is, since we, with our bare hands,
captured this quarry and tore its bleeding body
limb from limb.[11]

With her vision clouded by her pride in her achievements, Agave rejoices in the fact that she no longer is engaged in traditional female pursuits:

I have left my shuttle
at the loom; I raised my sight to higher things—
to hunting animals with my bare hands.[12]

Agave represents woman in an Amazonian state. Her Demetrian qualities have been repressed and the Dionysiac have triumphed to such an extent that she is unable to remember that she is a mother. Or identify that the "animal" she has rent apart with her bare hands is her own son. So why should any society place any importance upon the value of the Mother? Matriarchy, for Bachofen, has now been placed in such a position that it, in turn, degrades the male:

the new form, beneath the sheen of a rich material and intellectual life, concealed a diminished vitality, a moral decay, which contributed more than any other cause to the decline of the ancient world. Masculine bravery went hand in hand with the older matriarchy; the Dionysian matriarchy weakened and degraded men to such a degree that the women came to despise them.[13]

Whether or not Bachofen was justified in making these claims for a matriarchal system that had been in place, one can at least compare the behavior of Demeter, in her search for her daughter, to that of Agave. The result of this comparison is to see two completely different mothers. One mother nurturing, protecting, fighting and, eventually, winning the battle for the right of return for her daughter. Demeter, and humanity, undergo great suffer-

[11] Euripides, op. cit., 1206–1209.
[12] Ibid., 1236–1238.
[13] Bachofen, op. cit., 103.

ing in her struggle with the Olympian gods to achieve her daughter's return. We are readily able to describe Agave, who is also a mother, as a besotted, self-centered woman. She is besotted with her ability to kill, with her following of Dionysus, with her misplaced role as a hunter, and her own perception of her greatness. So full of hubris is she that Agamemnon himself would be outshone. But perhaps it is still correct to call Agave mother, for her capacity for destruction is shared by the Great Mother as well as the Feminine Archetype.

> But the elementary character of the Archetypal Feminine is far from containing only positive features. Just as the Great Mother can be terrible as well as good, so the Archetypal Feminine is not only a giver and protector of life but, as container, also holds fast and takes back; she is the goddess of life and death at once. As the symbol of the black-and-white egg indicates, the Feminine contains opposites, and the world actually lives because it combines.[14]

Agave certainly represents both life and death, as she has given birth to her son and then taken his life. Nevertheless this is not the emphasis Euripides places upon her actions. Rather it is the murderous aspect that he stresses, to the detriment of bearing life.

Aristotle, whose massive output of work so greatly influenced the Western world, continues the downgrading of the female, especially the female as mother. In *On The Generation of Animals*, Aristotle makes the following statement:

> the female always provides the material, the male that which fashions it, for this is the power that we say they each possess, and this is what is meant by calling them male and female. . . . While the body is from the female, it is the soul that is from the male, for the soul is the reality of a particular body.[15]

And he elaborates further concerning the importance of the male in the act of creation: "Hence in such animals the male

---

[14] Neumann, op. cit., 45.

[15] Aristotle, *Biological Treatises*, trans. Platt, ii., chap. 4, 1952, Encyclopaedia Britannica, Chicago, 279.

always perfects the work of generation, for he imparts the sensitive soul, either by means of the semen, or without it."[16] We will ignore the further arguments regarding the allocation of the sex of the child and how this may be achieved—tying of one teste, whether the wind is in the North or the South, whether old or young men produce more female children, whether more male children are born deformed because "the male is much superior to the female in natural heat," causing it to move around in the womb and thus cause damage—and concentrate on the statement that the male is responsible for the soul of the infant and that the female is only responsible for the body. Aristotle's use of the word "soul" relates it to the body, perhaps the life force. In this he is distancing himself from Plato. In this book I have used "soul" to signify the mutable part of the human composite, as does Aristotle, but "spirit" to signify the immutable, which is a more Platonic reading. What is important concerning Aristotle's views on the creation of life is the utter insignificance of any input by the female. As Radford Reuther explains it, Aristotelian thought influenced Christianity through "the teachings of Thomas Aquinas, who remains the normative theologian for the Roman Catholic tradition."[17] This teaching aligns woman with imperfection, unfit for any role of governance, thereby making it necessary for her to be governed by a male at all times.

These depictions of the feminine that I see as descending from the *Iliad* portray the woman as feckless, untrustworthy, brainless, not worthy of training in any sphere except cleaning and providing sustenance, representative of the dark injustices that spring from chthonic beliefs, and finally, to be thought of as only the receptacle for the seed of man. In short, she is a requirement for the gestation and rearing of children. Keeping her "barefoot and pregnant" was a belief present then and, for many, still today. From Hesiod's misogynist belief that all the evils in the world were loosed upon it by a woman's actions to Aristotle's [false] theory that

---

[16] Aristotle, *Biological Treatises*, op. cit., ii., chap. 5, 282.
[17] Radford Reuther, *Women, Religion and Sexuality*, op. cit. (55, n. 25).

every male seed would normally produce a male. Females are born only through a defect in gestation in which the male seed fails to fully form the female matter. The result is a defective human being or woman.[18]

There was the very weak solution offered by Aeschylus to the problem of a woman killing her husband, leading on to the downright hatred of humanity displayed by Euripides. These examples follow on from the *Iliad,* where even the most warmly depicted woman, Andromache, is still only a chattel, and Helen—the prize being fought for—calls herself "worthless." The importance of woman as mother is suppressed by this chain of thought. The repression of woman becomes institutionalized by this type of thinking, from whatever source. As Radford Ruether has shown, Christianity, through Aquinas, has adopted much of this. Woman is forced into the position of subordination. Of course, the soul is subordinate to the spirit, but somehow the belief that male and female alike possess both soul and spirit is lost.

★★★

To return to the treatment of women in the *Odyssey,* let me first say that no treatment is universally applied. We must remember the treatment of the maidservants, hanging in a row like so many felons. But these were not Odysseus's instructions to Telemachus, who is still a young man with the black and white outlook we all possess in our youth. Odysseus, the mature male who has been reborn, sets the punishment for the suitors and the maidservants because they have offended against his name, his family, and in particular his wife, who has no defence but her cunning, and against the ideals of womanhood she represents. The punishment is death, but it was to be death by sword for the maids. Telemachus claims this death by hanging to be more appropriate as punishment for the manner in which his mother was treated, but it appears more as if the callow youth is repaying his own perceived slights. Therefore we must dismiss the actions of Telemachus as unimportant to the argument. Consider instead the relationship between Odysseus and Penelope, or Alcinous and Arete, splendid

---

[18] Aristotle, op. cit., 22.

examples of *hieros gamos*, and the relationship between Penelope, Arete and their respective children. Remembering these, are we able to see the pattern repeated in *The Hymn to Demeter?*

The cult of Isis existed before our record of Demeter and was contemporaneous with the Greek myth. The Isis myth clearly sets out her role:

> the fullest account of the myth of Isis and Osiris extant in Egyptian sources . . . was inscribed on a limestone stela dating from the Eighteenth Dynasty (1567–1320 BC). This myth emphasizes Isis's role as protector of the pharaohs in that she guards Osiris while he is the living king, gives him new life when he is dead, and conceives a legitimate heir, their son Horus.[19]

Is the Eleusian cult merely an Attic version of an older myth? Goblet D'Alviella, in his introduction, states that as far as is known: "The Mysteries encompassed ten centuries and like all institutions, they have, to some extent, been subjected to the law of change."[20] The law of change must govern all material life, and it is in the material world that the worship of Demeter takes place. This does not mean that the essential qualities of the Mother Goddess change necessarily, but the manner in which she is recognized does. The story of Demeter appears to be of a victory over the Olympian Gods, and for some time she has control over the three spheres—life, death, and life hereafter—in the telling of the tale. But my argument is that this is the last flowering of the worship of the goddess in any major way in Greek culture. In Greek thought her position is eventually usurped by an Olympian male god, Dionysus. The worship of the goddess is never again as important as at this time and even this importance is fleeting. Nevertheless the myth does not die. The myth attracts us because it answers a need that society does not necessarily acknowledge.

A simple reading of the myth of Demeter and Persephone will see the symbol of birth in the cycle of the seasons and their union

[19] Serinity Young, *An Anthology of Sacred Texts By and About Women*, 1993, Hammersmith, London, HarperCollins, 128.

[20] Goblet D'Alviella, *The Mysteries of Eleusis*, 1981, England, The Aquarian Press, 7.

with the earth, which allows the flowering of the vegetation. Birth is coupled with recognition of death in Persephone's sojourn underground, which is symbolized by the seed in the earth or storeroom waiting to germinate. In this reading, Persephone returns from her sojourn underground and remains above ground for nine months of the year, a gestation period that allows life on earth to live again. She is, in fact, reborn each year to life on the material plane in the same manner as the crops of corn. Just as a portion of the corn crop must be set aside for seed and next year's crop, so Persephone and Demeter must give up some part of their relationship, each year, to symbolize and make apparent that there will be a further year's crop and, more importantly, to signify return. Eliade says that among settled people acknowl-edgement of their staple food supply is sometimes connected "with a mythical drama involving sexual union, death, and resur-rection."[21] The divine link between cereal crop, humanity, resur-rection, and Persephone is Demeter. Persephone signifies the soul as does Demeter the spirit. She, Persephone, is the maker of man-ifestation, causing the corn to grow, and represents the soul that remains in the terrestrial body; or conversely, the Underworld where Persephone resides is the material world, the world of Uri-zen that we all inhabit. The soul ascends to Olympus with the Spirit and returns to Hades/Earth as a seed. Both plant and human energies are directed towards reaching for the sky, or Olympus. They are vegetative and spiritual co-ordinates. Thus the Hymn is much more than an agricultural myth or a myth con-cerning the relationship between daughter and mother.

While the *Hymn to Demeter* is found within the *Homeric Hymns*, the worship of the Mother Goddess behind this story is much older. In the area around the Mediterranean this story links to the earliest references of the Mother Goddess and most surely predate the myths that contain references to a pantheon of sky gods headed by a male. Swami Satyananda tells us of the importance of the worship of the Mother Goddess in the Hindu religion:

---

[21] Eliade, *A History of Religious Ideas*, op. cit., i., 39–40.

The Divine Mother is the symbolic power behind creation, preservation and dissolution. The whole universe is the manifestation of this power. Devi is synonymous with Shakti or the Divine power that manifests, sustains and transforms the universe as the one unifying force of existence. Since Shakti cannot be worshipped in its essential nature, it is worshipped as we conceive of it.[22]

The empowerment that is demonstrated in the Demetrian myth through the agency of Persephone, and the link between life and death, is as Shakti, as Devi. As in the Hindu tradition the triadic nature of the Divine Mother is repeated in *The Hymn to Demeter*. Demeter, in her search for Persephone, is informed by Hecate. Helene Foley tells us:

> In later myth and cult, Hekate is strongly associated with both goddesses, becoming at times virtually identical with them. . . .
> In some versions of the myth, Hekate is said to be Demeter's daughter or to have gone to the underworld to search for Persephone, in others, she was identified with Persephone.[23]

Demeter is the symbol for motherhood in the Greek tradition from the Homeric period, and she descends from a long line of Earth goddesses who are not necessarily Greek but, instead, answer and explain an important need in the human psyche. The hymn is an ongoing celebration of the Mother Goddess, but it is, more particularly, the beginning of the end of its long history. Demeter's victory, when she single-handedly takes on the entire pantheon of Olympian gods, may be seen as heroic, but ends in

---

[22] Sivananda and Satyananda Saraswati, op. cit., 13.

[23] Helene P. Foley, *The Homeric Hymn to Demeter*, trans. Foley, 1994, Princeton, Princeton University Press, 124. Foley questions whether Demeter is endeavoring to defeat the male hierarchy with her attempt to immortalize Demophoon: "In her anger at Zeus, Demeter defies the boundary between gods and mortals in trying to make the mortal Demophoon immortal. Is she also, like Hera, trying to produce an immortal male champion who will challenge Zeus?" [113] But Demeter, the spirit who has lost her soul, may well be attempting to produce another soul.

the absorption of Demetrian motherhood by the paternalistic sky gods. This is done at a cost to the feminine, but as Bachofen states of the Dionysiac religion: "this religion, which developed the male principle at the expense of womanhood, did more than any other to degrade man below the level of woman."[24]

In the Hymn, Demeter's status is that of Queen of the World, which is the Underworld, through her daughter, Persephone, and of the Heavens by virtue of the promise made to her by Zeus. Her formidable position has to be reduced, and this occurs with the rise of Dionysus. Demeter, like Mary, was true to the expectations of her society, and her role was altered to meet the needs of that society. The resolution of her status, and her subsequent replacement by Dionysus, allowed the absorption of an earlier chthonic religion into that of the newer Olympian religion. This is the pendulum swing that Bachofen says takes place when one rule supplants another that had previously held the unassailable despotic position.

The reconciliation with or denial of the material, chthonic gods, linked with generation both in humanity and nature and of which "woman stands at the summit,"[25] is achieved by the supplanting of Demeter by Dionysus. Demeter, whose story extends back into pre-history, is forgotten, even though the worship of both deities is concurrent for some time. Leeming and Page support the feminist point of view and see the change as the rise of patriarchy. In this view they are in agreement with Bachofen.

> Finally, it can be said that the Demeter-Persephone myth answered a need for the feminine in the spiritual realm once Goddess gave way to God. This was a need suggested by the great popularity of the Demeter mysteries in patriarchal Greece, in spite of the official religion. The same need would give rise later to the popular cult of the Virgin in Christianity.[26]

One could not deny a need for the feminine in the spiritual realm

---

[24] Bachofen, op. cit., 100.

[25] Ibid., 186.

[26] Leeming and Page, op. cit., 67.

nor that that need was answered in Greece, for a time, by the myth of Demeter and Persephone. But it is the equilibrium of Empedocles, or the wedded contrarieties of Blake, which makes the spiritual accessible to all, male and female, and not the supremacy of either the maternal or paternal god.

Coomaraswamy, like Blake, sees the need for both male and female in the equation and quotes A. B. Cook in the following:

> Zeus as sky-father is in essential relation to an earth-mother. Her name varies from place to place and from time to time . . . everywhere and always either patent or latent, the earth-mother is there as the necessary correlative and consort of the sky-father.[27]

Zeus too is the "necessary correlative," the masculine spirit opposite to and in conjunction with the feminine soul. This is the ideal under which we should operate. Leeming and Page are right in assuming that this is lost, but not correct in the assumption that one must replace the other in order to achieve balance. Balance is never achieved if one half of the seesaw is weighted.

But for Swami Satyananda Saraswati, what has occurred in the major religions is that either one or the other spiritual tradition forms the basis of their understanding:

> In the vedic tradition, it is said that the feminine divine power is the ultimate power. Jagatmata, the mother of the world, is the ultimate reality. In tantra, Shakti is the primal energy responsible for creation. All cultures of the ancient world worshipped the principles of shakti and shiva. . . . There are two spiritual traditions existing in the world: one is matriarchal and the other is patriarchal. Matriarchal traditions speak of God as the universal mother, the goddess, the force of nature. According to the patriarchal traditions, God the creator is a father, not a mother. Judaism, Christianity and Islam are patriarchal. Tantra, Hinduism, Buddhism,

---

[27] Coomaraswamy, *Traditional Art*, op. cit., n.4, 354. Coomaraswamy is quoting Arthur Bernard Cook, *Zeus; A Study in Ancient Religion*, 3 vols. (Cambridge 1914–1940), i. 779.

Zoroastrianism, Shintoism, Taoism and the Native American traditions are matriarchal traditions.[28]

In both the Vedic and Tantric traditions the "feminine power is the ultimate power." As evidenced by the *Hymn,* this was also the case in the early Greek tradition and then lost. What is singular concerning this myth is the central role played by two feminine figures. The American Plains Indians have two female figures in their mythology, balanced by two male figures.[29] Demeter and Persephone share these links with the earth, but they are also the same feminine power that underlies Vedic and Tantric traditions, the principles of Shakti and Shiva.

In Chapter Two of her book, Radford Ruether looks at the Goddess in the Ancient Mediterranean.

> All of these goddesses are closely related to a beloved . . . who is connected with food production or rain in the face of threatened drought and whose resurrection, through the intervention of the goddess, restores life to the earth.[30]

There is no doubt that Demeter fulfills the requirements stated above. She loves her daughter, and that desire for reunion with her is so powerful that food production ceases until the union takes place. With just this much of the myth it is easy to see why Bachofen chose Demeter as the symbol of motherhood. The other three goddesses—Inanna/Ishtar, Anat, and Isis—have male consorts or lovers. The singularity of the Demeter and Persephone myth raises some questions. Was Bachofen right in designating this as an example of something much older? Are there grounds for believing that this proves the existence of a matriarchal society, or at the very least a matrilineal one whose myth is

---

[28] Sivananda and Satyananda Saraswati, op. cit., 27.

[29] Epes Brown, op. cit. (see 47, n.34]:

As in the distinction made within *Wakan-Tanka* between Grandfather and Father, so the Earth is considered under two aspects, that of Mother and Grandmother. The former is the earth considered as the producer of all growing forms, in act; whereas Grandmother refers to the ground or substance of all growing things-potentiality. This distinction is the same as that made by the Christian Scholastics between *natura naturans* and *natura naturata.*

[30] Radford Ruether, *Goddesses and the Divine Feminine,* 41.

absorbed into the paternalistic sky gods of Greece? Bachofen's point is that the *Hymn to Demeter* and the cult of Eleusis which followed (c. 1500 BC till the fifth century AD, according to Radford Ruether) were co-opted and absorbed by the followers of the sky god, Zeus. This seems quite apparent, particularly in the development of Dionysus, as the chthonic gods are replaced by the sky. He elaborates further on the value of the myth; even while it is being altered, "the legend becomes in its transformations a living expression of the stages in a people's development."[31] Thus any alteration caused by the values of the Olympian gods to the position of the Demetrian goddess strengthens Bachofen's belief that the earlier myth was of such power that it needed to be altered. To say only that this is patriarchal is to miss the degradation to the ideals of the society that were and still are occurring.

Foley makes the point that:

> Greek literature tends to link the female more strongly than the male with nature as opposed to culture, darkness as opposed to light, with periphery as opposed to the center, and with the ability to mediate among the spheres of nature, the gods and humankind.[32]

Certainly this appears to be so in this poem and in other literature. But *The Hymn to Demeter* also contradicts this reading. Most striking about this poem is not the showing of the mother and daughter link, the homage paid to the harvesting of grain, or whether this is a resolution regarding marriage,[33] but that the female, represented by Demeter and Persephone, possesses both soul and spirit and epitomizes the redemptive power that spirit possesses. The poem is redemptive in a manner that predates Christianity and is similar to the Cult of Isis. But it is redemption that is offered to any Greek speaker with the price of attending the rites—male, female, servant, and slave. More importantly this redemption is offered by the female acting as Spirit.

---

[31] Bachofen, op. cit., 74–75.

[32] Foley, *The Homeric Hymn to Demeter*, op. cit., 139.

[33] Ibid., 118–137. In this chapter Foley discusses the mother/daughter relationship and the possibility of changes being made between exogamous and endogamous marriage.

In Fragment XVIII, Parmenides (c. 500 BC) offers practical advice for achieving a harmonious, perhaps even a "sacred," marriage and the creation of new life: "When a woman and man mix the seeds of Venus at the same time."[34] "At the same time" woman and man, both of equal importance, will participate in the act of love. The woman is not just a receptacle but an equal partner. But it is the female as guide to the path to knowledge which is of greater significance. Consider the importance of the female in Parmenides' "On Nature" poem. The horses are female, whether mares or fillies, and are led by maidens. The man who knows is set on the renowned way of the Daemon-goddess. The maidens are the Daughters of the Sun and they are leaving the abode of Night.[35] The goddess is Night, Νύξ, Nyx. Night, daughter of Chasm, is earlier sung of by Hesiod, "and then Aether and Day came forth from Night, who conceived and bore them after mingling in love with Erebos."[36] Michael Grant and John Hazel elaborate further on the power of Night and her protection of her son born by parthenogenesis:

> When Zeus was about to eject Hypnos from Olympus, Nyx protected her son and even the king of the gods had to yield.[37]

Through the gates of Night and Day, fitted with mighty doors that reach the sky, the man, Parmenides, is allowed to pass when Justice is gently persuaded by the maidens. He is then able to pass through the gates "filled by great doors And their changing keys

---

[34] Sworder, op. cit., 95.

[35] Peter Kingsley, *In the Dark Places of Wisdom*, 2008, Inverness CA, The Golden Sufi Centre, 49. Kingsley says the following:

> Every single figure Parmenides encounters in his poem is a woman or a girl. Even the animals are female, and he's taught by a goddess. The universe he describes is a feminine one; and if this man's poem represents the starting point for western logic, then something very strange has happened for logic to end up the way it has.

Kingsley elevates the role of the Goddess and denies the masculine principle. Blake's union, through Pity, of male and female is lost in this argument. From differing viewpoints, Bachofen and Doherty also do this. Equality between the sexes rather than the supremacy of either sex is a healthier position.

[36] Hesiod, *Theogony*, op. cit., 116–125.

[37] Grant and Hazel, *Who's Who in Classical Mythology*, op. cit., 234.

cruel Justice keeps."[38] Justice thus bars the way to further knowledge unless persuaded by the female guides of the male. Justice, Δίκη, like Night is a female god. Night tells him:

> You must discover all, both the unshaken heart of well rounded truth, and also the opinions of mortals in which there is no true trust.[39]

Thus "the man who knows" will learn to distinguish what is truth from untrustworthy opinion. The role played by Necessity is also of interest, 'Ανάγκη. The capitalization of this feminine noun draws attention to the role played by Necessity, who holds Being "in the bonds of limit."[40] But there is one further restrictive role played by the feminine, "For neither is there nor will there be anything besides Being, since Fate chained it to be whole and immobile."[41] Fate, Μοιρα, is another female goddess who appears to play a similar role in this poem to the role given to her in the *Iliad*.[42]

"The man who knows" has been set on his path—to further knowledge? redemption?—by the goddess. He travels in a chariot, which is towed by mares or fillies and accompanied by the daughters of the Sun, leaving the realm of Night, thus leaving darkness and traveling into light. Now he passes back through the doors into the palace of Night. These may be the doors that Hesiod tells us are both the source and the limits of the Earth.

> In front of these, Iapetus's son holds the broad sky with his head and tireless hands, standing immovable, where Night and Day passing near greet one another as they cross the great bronze threshold. The one is about to go in and the

[38] Sworder, op. cit., 191.

[39] Ibid., 191.

[40] Ibid., 193.

[41] Ibid.

[42] Edith Hamilton, *Mythology*, 1969, New York, Mentor Books, New American Library, 27. Hamilton is speaking of Zeus's strengths in the extract:

Nevertheless he was not omnipotent or omniscient, either. He could be opposed and deceived. Poseidon dupes him in the *Iliad* and so does Hera. Sometimes, too, the mysterious power, Fate, is spoken of as stronger than he. Homer makes Hera ask him scornfully if he proposes to deliver from death a man Fate has doomed.

other is going out the door, and never does the house hold
them both inside, but always the one goes out from the
house and passes over the earth, while the other in turn
remaining inside the house waits for the time of her own
departure, until it comes. The one holds much-seeing light
for those on the earth, but the other holds Sleep in her
hands, the brother of Death—deadly Night, shrouded in
murky cloud.[43]

These bronze doors pictured by Hesiod are both source and
limit. Those shown by Parmenides are also the gates to the heart
which are moved by the emotion of Pity as described by Blake,
the place where God is found for Meister Eckhart,[44] and for
Guénon: "the place of union of the individual with the Universal."[45] This is the ultimate aim for Parmenides, Eckhart, Guénon,
and Blake. For Blake it is through an emotion which he designates as belonging to the feminine, for Parmenides it is when
"much punishing Justice" relents with the help of the feminine
through the goddesses. But for all it is "union of the individual
with the Universal."

Plato (c. 428–347 BC), given that his main voice is masculine,
may seem to be a strange choice in the support of women. Yet
there is much of value to be found in his work with regard to
women. In the *Timaeus* we find some contrasting views. Socrates
is the guest of honor in this discourse and merely recounts the
points he has already made in *The Republic*. After describing the
separation of the classes, husbandmen and artisans, from the
defenders of the state, the guardians, he then talks about their
education and pay. Next are the women:

> Neither did we forget the women; of whom we declared,
> that their natures should be assimilated and brought into
> harmony with those of the men, and that common pursuits
> should be assigned to them both in time of war and in their
> ordinary life.[46]

---

[43] Hesiod, *Theogony*, op. cit., 746–757.
[44] Underhill, quoting Meister Eckhart, op. cit. (see 37, n.31).
[45] Guénon, *Studies in Hinduism*, op. cit. (see 27, n. 74).
[46] Plato, *Timaeus*, tr. Jowett, 1952, Chicago, Encyclopaedia Britannica, 442.

That both men and women undertake common pursuits means that they are equally capable of undertaking these pursuits. Socrates then asks for a dialogue that will illustrate how their state, Athens, behaved well when victorious in war. Critias tells of Solon's trip to Egypt where he discovers the elders of Sais, who were admirers of the Greek way of government and also claimed Athene as their founder. They had records of Athens' history which went back 9,000 years and told how Athens defeated Atlantis. Timaeus, of Locris in Italy, is to start the dialogue because he "is the most of an astronomer amongst us, and has made the nature of the universe his special study."[47] Timaeus proceeds with the telling of the formation of the universe. His treatment of women is not as even-handed as that of his listener.

> He who lived well during his appointed time was to return and dwell in his native star, and there he would have a blessed and congenial existence. But if he failed in attaining this, at the second birth he would pass into a woman, and if, when in that state of being, he did not desist from evil, he would continually be changed into some brute who resembled him in the evil nature he had acquired.[48]

Timaeus's special study of the universe and the creation myth which he proposes has not allowed him to reach the same level of equanimity with which Socrates regards women. Plato stresses and emphasizes this difference with this concluding statement.

> On the subject of animals, then, the following remarks may be offered. Of the men who came into the world, those who were cowards or led unrighteous lives may with reason be supposed to have changed into the nature of women in the second generation.[49]

This very long dialogue delivered by a non-Greek may have allowed Plato to make statements he would not put into the mouth of Socrates. It is answered by the unfinished dialogue of

[47] Plato, *Timaeus*, op. cit., 446–447.
[48] Ibid., 453.
[49] Ibid., 476.

Critias. Again the ideal state as described by Socrates is mirrored in the description of early Athens as is the role of women.

> Moreover, since military pursuits were then common to men and women, the men of those days in accordance with the custom of the time set up a figure and image of the goddess in full armour, to be a testimony that all animals which associate together, male as well as female, may, if they please, practise in common the virtue which belongs to them without the distinction of sex.[50]

As these dialogues go together, we may well assume that Plato meant us to balance these arguments. Or, maybe we are to see just how strange the man from Locris actually was. Perhaps a reading of another argument may resolve this issue. I have said that there was a recapitulation of the arguments put forward in *The Republic*, but perhaps a more thorough reading will help clarify Plato's position in relation to women. As always, Socrates enters into a logical discussion regarding the abilities of men versus women.

> There is therefore no function in society which is peculiar to woman as woman or man as man; natural abilities are similarly distributed in each sex, and it is natural for women to share all occupations with men, though in all women will be the weaker partners.[51]

All have the same natural abilities: the ability to think, to reason, to ascend to the same spiritual understanding of the cosmos and, to a lesser extent, females will be able to share in the physical work. Socrates has already made the point that the females will not be quite so strong, but that "if we are going to use men and women for the same purposes, we must teach them the same things."[52] He clarifies this even further:

> Then if men and women as a class appear to be qualified for different occupations, we shall assign them different occupations accordingly; but if the only difference apparent

---

[50] Plato, *Critias*, trans. Jowett, 1952, Chicago, Encyclopaedia Britannica, 480.
[51] Plato, *The Republic*, trans. Lee, ed. Rieu, op. cit., 209.
[52] Ibid., 204.

between them is that the female bears and the male begets, we shall not admit that this is a difference relevant for our purpose, but shall still maintain that our male and female guardians ought to follow the same occupations.[53]

Accordingly, the only difference between male and female is their ability to do the tasks they are assigned. Such clarity deserved more recognition! Some males will be better at the tasks than some females, and some females will be better than some males, and the only judgement will be based upon their respective and individual ability.

We have a record of one such female who achieved this equality:

> Hypatia (370–415 CE) of Alexandria was a well known and highly regarded Neoplatonist. She equalled her father Theon in his fame as a mathematician and astronomer, and she publicly taught, both in Athens and Alexandria, these subjects as well as the philosophy of Plato and Aristotle.[54]

Hypatia's ability was not recognized by the Christian Church. Through the agency of the Bishop of Alexandria, Cyril, she was put to death by a mob.

Plato honors the feminine still further in his dialogue *The Symposium*, an encomium on Love. The various dinner guests speak on this subject, commencing with Phaedrus, then Pausanias, Eryximachus, Aristophanes, Agathon, and finally Socrates. Plato shows us the differing views on Love from the respective speakers, and his touch is very sure, even comical when Aristophanes is speaking of the three sexes. Then, to conclude the discussion, Alcibiades pours out a paean of love for Socrates. Socrates' account links love with both the beautiful and the good and he explains that Diotima of Mantineia, "a woman wise in this and in many other kinds of knowledge . . . was my instructress in the art of love."[55] Diotima instructs Socrates in the manner he uses to instruct his listeners, so that it appears Socrates learnt more

---

[53] Plato, *Republic*, op. cit., 208.
[54] Young, op. cit., 177.
[55] Plato, *Symposium*, trans. Jowett, op. cit., 163.

than the art of love from this wise woman. When she asks him "What is the cause, Socrates, of love, and the attendant desire?"[56] he tells her: "But I have told you already, Diotima, that my ignorance is the reason why I come to you; for I am conscious that I want a teacher."[57]

Diotima's answer is Platonic, comparing the immortality that most attain through their children with the pregnant soul:

> But souls that are pregnant—for there certainly are men who are more creative in their souls than in their bodies— conceive that which is proper for the soul to conceive or contain. And what are these conceptions?—wisdom and virtue in general. . . . But the greatest and fairest sort of wisdom by far is that which is concerned with the ordering of states and families, and which is called temperance and justice.[58]

From here the soul must progress, having used the physical world as a means of understanding, to appreciation of the essence of beauty which is unchanging and immortal. If man has eyes to see this,

> he will be enabled to bring forth, not images of beauty, but realities (for he has hold not of an image but of a reality), and bringing forth and nourishing true virtue to become the friend of God and be immortal, if mortal man may.[59]

Thus a woman instructs a man on those most serious of topics, how to live one's life in wisdom and virtue and attain knowledge of the unchanging Good. Beautiful, drunken Alcibiades then speaks to the group, and his speech reifies Socrates' position, learnt from Diotima, concerning Love. He speaks of his attempts to seduce Socrates, and how they were of no avail. Socrates' eyes, like those of Blake, were fixed on another world more real than the passions of this world. And the means of attaining this reality was taught by a woman.

---

[56] Plato, *Symposium*, op, cit.
[57] Ibid.
[58] Ibid., 167.
[59] Plato, *Republic*, op, cit.

THE FORCE OF TENDERNESS

The more esoteric aspects of the monotheistic religions allow a softer approach to the feminine than the rigid thinking we see in orthodox thought. As Young illustrates, Judaism has its Kabbala:

> The main ideas of these teachings center on the mystical and secret nature of God and the complex relationship that exists between God, humanity, and the world. An important aspect of these relationships is Shekhinah, a female term often translated as wisdom. While Shekhinah contains within itself this meaning of wisdom, frequently it is more specifically referred to as the manifestations of God, one of which is wisdom.[60]

From this we might draw the conclusion that Shekhinah occupies a role not unlike that described by Kabir:

> Knowledge is the branch, and the Name is the root.[61]

Offsetting the rigid rules governing male and female relationships in Judaism is this mystical teaching including "the commentary on Genesis 5, which emphasizes the simultaneous creation of male and female, drawing positive conclusions from this divine act."[62]

> *Rabbi Shim'on said*
> *"Male and female He created them."*
> *"High mysteries are revealed in these two verses.*
> *to make known the Glory on high*
> *the mystery of faith*
> *Out of this mystery, Adam was created..."*

---

[60] Young, op. cit., 28. The *Zohar* is one of the main texts of the international religious movement of Judaism known as Kabbala. It was written in Spain by Moses de Leon (c.1240–1305) who attributed it to Shimeon ben Yohai, a second-century Palestinian mystic. The text is a mystical commentary on the first five books of the Hebrew Bible and was mainly studied by a small esoteric group until the expulsion of the Jews from Spain in 1492. After this time the teachings of the Kabbala as expressed in the *Zohar* spread throughout the Jewish world.

[61] Kabir, op. cit. (LXXX) [see 43, n.22].

[62] Young, op. cit., 30.

From here we learn:
Out of this mystery, Adam was created "male and
*   female He created them;*
Any image that does not embrace male and female
*   is not a high and true image.*
We have established this in the mystery of our Mishnah."
(From *The Zohar,* 55–56)

"Any image that does not embrace male and female is not a high and true image." This is clearly the same message as Blake's "undivided Essence." From Judaism, Young demonstrates the link with the feminine in early Christianity.

> Pre-Pauline Christianity, sometimes referred to as the Jesus movement, was an egalitarian movement in which women figured prominently. The life of Jesus, as recorded in the gospels, brings out the importance of his mother Mary, his female disciples, and the many women he taught. As the tradition took shape, the role of women was reduced and the early equalitarian spirit was somewhat diminished.[63]

Young develops this with an acknowledgement of the development of religious communities for women "in the early part of the thirteenth century, especially the Beguines."[64] On a more esoteric level, Gnosticism had a creation myth which was

> probably composed c.400 CE in Alexandria. It incorporates parts of the Genesis story, but from a Gnostic point-of-view. Primarily it emphasizes the role of Sophia, wisdom, both at the beginning of creation and as a means of salvation. It is she who gives Adam breath, a soul, and her daughter, Eve, to be his instructor. The forces of delusion, in the form of seven archangels, interfere violently in order to keep

[63] Young, op. cit., 63:

This is not a process unique to Christianity, other religions such as Buddhism and many smaller religious movements begin with the teachings of a charismatic male who attracts a large number of active and vocal female followers. Generally these movements challenge the norms of their society and when the founder dies, in order to survive, the movement usually modifies its more radical views and begins to conform to their society's practices, especially with regard to women.

[64] Ibid.

humans in ignorance and tell Adam and Eve not to eat from the Tree of Knowledge. The myth also describes the eventual conquest of the forces of darkness by the forces of light, especially wisdom.[65]

Along with the Gospel of Mary, another Gnostic document, this is a softening of the rigid position of a male-dominated religion. And there is of course Mary, Mother of God and Mater Misericordia. Young has this to say about the enduring popularity of the Angelus:

> The pervasiveness of Mary's popularity among Christians is partly shown by the custom of the Angelus. During the Middle Ages the recitation of three Hail Marys three times a day as part of the Angelus became popular. Church bells would ring out in the morning, at noon, and in the evening, calling the faithful to prayer.[66]

She also notes the enduring response to the Hail Mary and how it was incorporated into the Angelus, the bell that was heard on a regular basis in the Catholic Church.

> The best known and most frequent prayer to Mary is the Hail Mary, the first part of which is taken from the words of the angel who announces Mary's conception in the Gospel of Luke. As such it was in use quite early and became a frequent prayer in Europe by the twelfth century. The second part, the supplication, was added around the fifteenth century. The simplicity of this prayer contributed to its popularity. It states Mary's uniqueness as the Mother of God and seeks her intercession for eternal salvation.[67]

---

[65] Young, op. cit., 41.
[66] Ibid., 63–64.
[67] Ibid:

Hail, Mary,	Holy Mary,
full of grace,	Mother of God,
the Lord is with you.	pray for us sinners,
Blessed are you among women	now and at the hour of our death
and blessed is the fruit of your	
womb, Jesus.	

In Islamic belief also Young sees a pattern of acknowledgment of women's power:

> In effect, the first level of Islam, the great tradition of ortho-doxy, is almost exclusively in the hands of men and is author-itative for both men and women while a second level, the folk tradition of Islam, which is of less certain orthodoxy, is primarily in the hands of women, though some men are involved. This folk tradition also has an impact on the lives of both women and men. While men control the lives of women through orthodoxy women can control or at least coerce men through the folk tradition. For instance, Muslim men seem to be particularly wary of the magical procedures available to women. Checks and balances exist that give Muslim women a degree of control over their lives in a way that is not apparent in the orthodox system of Islam.[68]

The Islamic folk tradition does not seem to be as formulated as Judaism or Christianity and bears some relation to the thought of the Plains Indians, where the feminine has the connotation of magical power:

> She should know, further, that each month when her period arrives she bears an influence with which she must be care-ful, for the presence of a woman in this condition may take away the power of a holy man.[69]

Unfortunately the magical power of the female is something all too often abhorred by the opposite sex. Though the Iliadic line is apparent in the treatment of the female sex in the orthodoxy of the monotheistic religions, all three are tempered by the strand I claim starts with the *Odyssey*. That this imbalance is redressed in some part by the Odyssean line is to humanity's advantage. The empowerment of one sex over another—and it is of no conse-quence which sex it is—is not only a reduction in the subjugated sex but also in that of the ruler. It is always retrograde.

In the second century AD, Pausanias, tells us of the Altar of Pity which is present in the agora:

---

[68] Young, op. cit., 95.
[69] Epes Brown, *The Sacred Pipe*, op. cit. (see 47, n.33).

Among the things in the market of Athens not well known to everyone is the Altar of Pity.[70]

The word he uses is Ἐλέου, Pity, and it is the name of a god:

The Athenians are the only Greeks who pay honours to this very important god in human life and human reverses.[71]

So important is this god that the Altar of Pity was, as archaeology tells us, built on the site of the Altar of the Twelve Gods. Perhaps more fittingly for the concept of pity in this thesis, however, is the description given by Statius, c. AD 45–95, in his epic on Thebes:[72]

There was in the midst of the city an altar belonging to no god of power: gentle Clemency had there her seat, and the wretched made it sacred; never lacked she a new suppliant, none did she condemn or refuse their prayers. All that ask are heard, night and day may one approach and win the heart of the goddess by complaints alone.[73]

Here the god is female and there are no rituals between the supplicant and the deity.

Around is a grove of gentle trees, marked by the cult of the venerable, wool-entwined laurel and the suppliant olive. No image is there, to no metal is the divine form entrusted, in hearts and minds does the goddess delight to dwell.[74]

Images, or metal statues, are not necessary to know this goddess, but in the heart and mind of the supplicant does she dwell. This is the transcendent pity of Blake.

---

[70] Pausanias, *Guide to Greece*, Vol. 1, trans. Levi, 1979, Middlesex, Penguin Books, i. 17:1.

[71] Ibid., i. 17:1.

[72] The link between Pity and Clemency in the English language may be shown by the following extracts from *The New Shorter Oxford English Dictionary*, 2 Vols., 1993, Oxford, Clarendon Press: clemency: 1. mildness or gentleness of temper in the exercise of authority of power; mercy, leniency from the Latin *clementia*. mercy: (O) Fr. *merci* f.L. *mercei*, *merced-* reward, wages, revenue, in Chr.L. used for *misericordia* pity.

[73] Statius, II, *Thebaid*, trans. Mozley, MCMLXIX, Harvard, Harvard University Press, 481–486.

[74] Statius, *Thebaid*, 491–494.

Conclusion

THE ROLES of the female in pre-history and her connections to the physical world through birth and death have shown us that, when not revered, her worth was recognized and celebrated. In the *Iliad* the mortal women are more often portrayed as a means of comfort or a prize for valor. As a female prize, Briseis's lament allows us some insight into how she feels. Does Achilles reciprocate and really feel some affection towards Briseis? If he does, it is not shown. As Briseis's lament is for Patroclus as advocate, her sorrow may well be for her own situation. Acknowledgment of the maternal role is shown only in the defeated Trojans through Hecuba and Andromache. The importance of the mother and the gift she brings of children is dismissed as secondary in the Iliadic world. The goddesses in the *Iliad* display the same potency as the gods, being often equal to them in strength and shrewdness—particularly Athene and Hera, who both demonstrate maternal protective instincts in their advancement of the Greek cause. Aphrodite is protective of her son, Aeneas. When Zeus wavers concerning the deaths of Sarpedon and Hector, his hesitation is quickly countered by the intervention of Hera and then Athene. Dismissing Hera as manipulative—a shrew or a nag—is an easy option. This description of her has a masculine bias. Her manipulation of Zeus, using the attributes of Aphrodite, is no different to Zeus's manipulation of Aphrodite using the same method:

> Aphrodite so often inflicted helpless love on the other gods, including of course Zeus, that Zeus in retaliation made her suffer the humiliation of falling in love with a cowherd, Anchises, so that she might know what it was like to be tormented with desire for a mortal.[1]

---

[1] Jenny March, *The Penguin Book of Classics*, 2008, London, Penguin, 12.

It is more likely that all women and all men have used these same techniques when required.

Hesiod makes woman the cause of all problems and evils, although she is created by Zeus and accepted by

> mistaken-minded Epimetheus (Afterthought)—he who turned out to be an evil from the beginning for men who live on bread, for he was the one who first accepted Zeus' fabricated woman, the maiden.[2]

Hesiod's tale reinforces the Iliadic view. Aeschylus's argument—that woman is merely the receptacle for the seed and that she contributes nothing else—demonstrates that the importance of the Mother Goddess has vanished. It appears that Aeschylus is merely echoing a perceived wisdom of the time, for Clytemnestra is one of the greatest dramatic creations of a powerful woman. This cannot be said of Euripides. These perceptions regarding women—as a comforter, a valor prize, a purveyor of every nasty thing that may happen to a man, and without any influence upon the child she carries—are still current beliefs for many.

By contrast, the Odyssean line is quite different. Penelope is the representative of the virtuous mortal woman. Although still circumscribed by the rules governing women in her society, she nevertheless tests the boundaries of those rules in her effort to retain and protect her place as Odysseus's wife and mother of Telemachus. Queen Arete, whose community shows respect for the equality of the sexes, is both mother and wise woman. In the *Odyssey,* the goddesses guide, instruct, and protect Odysseus. Athene mothers Odysseus until the confrontation with the suitors. Then, like a mother teaching her child to walk, she stands back and he realizes he is on his own. More importantly, in the *Odyssey* there is an emphasis on marriage, marriage that has as its aim *hieros gamos*—and this we have directly from Odysseus when he addresses Nausicaa:

> And for yourself, may the gods grant you all your heart desires, a husband and a home, and may they bestow on you as well oneness of heart in all its excellence. For noth-

---

[2] Hesiod, *Theogony,* op. cit., 511–514.

ing is greater or better than this, than when a man and a woman keep house together sharing one heart and mind, a great grief to their foes and a joy to their friends; while their own fame is unsurpassed.[3]

The mother and daughter relationship encapsulates the spirit mothering the soul in *The Hymn to Demeter*. In Parmenides' fragments, the feminine is also of importance to "the man who knows." Like the goddesses who surround and protect Odysseus, the feminine guides and instructs him. Plato, apart from the odd thoughts by Timaeus which he counters with very different points of view by Socrates and Critias, states that women have as much capacity to be guardians as men, providing they receive the necessary education. Women are as educable as men. And it is a wise woman who instructs Socrates about Love, which inspires and sustains him on his life's journey. The portrayal of the feminine in this Odyssean line is quite distinctly different to the Iliadic. The role of the feminine exceeds the purely physical. She is often the path to knowledge, the educator or expediter, or simply, and more importantly, the equivalence.

A simplistic reading of the significance of soul and spirit allows for the female to be reduced merely to the mortal realm:

Male † Spirit † immutability
Female † Soul † mutability

When this occurs in an organized fashion, then all the undesirable things of this world will belong to the female. While true that the female has far stronger links to the material world, especially the links to birth and death, there is one major error in this argument—failure to acknowledge that male and female each contain within them soul and spirit. Each human being contains within them the "other" too. This is revealed by what takes place in the more esoteric and mystical interpretations.

Blake breaks this simplification by giving the emotion of pity to the feminine emanation.[4] Pity has been treated with respect in various cultures, but not in quite the same manner as by Blake.

[3] *Od.VI*:180–185.
[4] *K*.328–329, *FZ*.336:360.

Athene protects and pities Odysseus. Demeter asks for pity but does not extend this to humanity, which suffers her pain as their own. Pausanias tells us that Pity, as a god, was honored in Athens two millennia ago. Statius offers us Clemency in the Latin world. The gods in the *Iliad* show pity towards the defeated Trojans. Achilles' behavior is softened by pity when Priam collects his son's corpse. Odysseus chides Eurycleia for rejoicing over the fallen suitors. Mary, Mother of God, personified as *Mater Misericordiae*, protects all, from bawd to bishop, who shelter under her blue cloak, the firmament. But for Blake, without pity there is no reunion with his god. Pity is the emotion that starts that process of union, and it is the emotion Blake allocates to the feminine. Through her and of her; this is the path all must follow, female and male.

www.ingramcontent.com/pod-product-compliance
Lightning Source LLC
Chambersburg PA
CBHW021505090426
42739CB00007B/470